Also by George Kalamaras

POETRY BOOKS

*Robert Desnos Finds His Sleep Medicines Beneath
Bachelard's Floorboards* (2024)
*To Sleep in the Horse's Belly: My Greek Poets
and the Aegean Inside Me* (2023)
*What My Hound Dog Is Scenting Through the Sloughgrass
Is a Way of Scenting Me* (2023)
Marsupial Mouth Movements (2021)
Through the Silk-Heavy Rains (2021)
We Slept the Animal: Letters from the American West (2021)
Luminous in the Owl's Rib (2019)
That Moment of Wept (2018)
The Hermit's Way of Being Human (2015)
Kingdom of Throat-Stuck Luck (2011)
The Recumbent Galaxy (with Alvaro Cardona-Hine) (2010)
Gold Carp Jack Fruit Mirrors (2008)
Even the Java Sparrows Call Your Hair (2004)
Borders My Bent Toward (2003)
The Theory and Function of Mangoes (2000)

POETRY CHAPBOOKS

Bootsie in the Bardo (2023)
The Shoes of the Fisherman's Wife Are Some Jive-Ass Slippers (2021)
The Mining Camps of the Mouth (2012)
Symposium on the Body's Left Side (2011)
Your Own Ox-Head Mask as Proof (2010)
The Scathering Sound (2009)
Something Beautiful Is Always Wearing the Trees (2009)
(with paintings by Alvaro Cardona-Hine)
Beneath the Breath (1988)
Heart Without End (1986)

CRITICAL STUDY

*Reclaiming the Tacit Dimension: Symbolic Form
in the Rhetoric of Silence* (1994)

The Rain That Doesn't Reach the Ground

GEORGE KALAMARAS

2025

DOS MADRES PRESS, INC.
P.O. Box 294, Loveland, Ohio 45140
www.dosmadres.com   editor@dosmadres.com

Dos Madres is dedicated to the belief that the small press is essential to the vitality of contemporary literature as a carrier of the new voice, as well as the older, sometimes forgotten voices of the past. And in an ever more virtual world, to the creation of fine books pleasing to the eye and hand.

Dos Madres is named in honor of Vera Murphy and Libbie Hughes, the "Dos Madres" whose contributions have made this press possible.

Dos Madres Press, Inc. is an Ohio Not For Profit Corporation and a 501 (c) (3) qualified public charity. Contributions are tax deductible.

Executive Editor: Robert J. Murphy

Illustration & Book Design: Elizabeth H. Murphy
www.illusionstudios.net

Front cover art: Garí, *Virga*, 1997, Oil on canvas, 38" x 54"

Author photo: "George and Blaisie," by Beth Blake

Typeset in Adobe Garamond Pro & Felix Titling
ISBN 978-1-962847-14-8
Library of Congress Control Number: 2024951105

First Edition
Copyright 2025 George Kalamaras
All rights reserved. No part of this book may be reproduced or transmitted in any form or by any means graphic, electronic or mechanical, including photo-copying, recording, taping or by any information storage or retrieval system, without the permission in writing from the publisher.
Published by Dos Madres Press, Inc.

for Mary Ann and Blaisie

*and for Mary Crow and Bill Tremblay,
who—forty-five years ago—
welcomed me open-armed to the West*

TABLE OF CONTENTS

TELL ME
Tell Me 1

ONE
THE WAY WEST
Beneath the Medicine Moon 5
The Way West 6
Winter Almanac 8
Train from Denver to Grand Junction 10
Drinking Tea in Mountain Moonlight,
    Trying to Think Only of Tea 12
Hibernation 16
Me. Mine. Moist. Exposed in the Medicine Bows 18
When Our Breath Overlaps with Ghosts 20
What the Moon Said 22
Driving Across the Great Plains 24
Only the Wind 26
Grasshopper and Cricket 27

TWO
THE SOMNAMBULIST DREAMS
Dream in Which Georgia O'Keeffe Is My Father 35

THREE
SOMETHING AKIN TO KIND BLOODLIGHT
Dead Grouse 39
Prayer to the Red Fox Who Appeared Near
    the August Blue Moon, 2023 41
At the Pawnee National Grasslands 43

Coyote Crossing the Road 44
Lamenting the Full Golden Moon
    Two Weeks Before It Breaks Itself in Two 46
Passing a Field of Antelope on Colorado County Road
    74E, Pondering the Darkness 47
Brain-Tanning the Hides 51
Time Was 53
Everything We'd Wanted to Say 54
Spoken Into 56
More Palomino, Please 58
Driving All Night from Here to There
    Is Sometimes Nowhere at All 60

FOUR
THE SOMNAMBULIST DREAMS

Dream in Which Cormac McCarthy Dreams
    He Is Dreaming Me Dreaming Him 65

FIVE
THE UNFORGIVING WAILING OF THE WIND-DRENCHED WIND

A Theory of Taxidermy 69
Drinking Coffee at the Only Bar in Dixon Because
    Richard Hugo, James Welch, and J. D. Reed
    Had Whiskey There 71
Big Timber, 1998 72
Graves at Victor 75
The Death of Nikola Tesla 79
At Fort Morgan 81
At the Abbey of St. Walburga, Virginia Dale, Colorado 83
The Long Death of Doc Holliday 85
501 Words West of Wichita 88
The Last Jump 90
Abandoned Cabin 93
The Mining Camps of the Mouth 95

SIX
THE SOMNAMBULIST DREAMS
Dream in Which John Haines and I Homestead
  Together in Alaska 99

SEVEN
NOCTURNE OF THE WESTERN NIGHT
Now That the Owls Have Gone 105
I Heard a Primitive Sadness from My Primordial
  Mouth 106
Rain All Night in the Rain 108
The Agony of the Leaves.. 110
When Lightning Bugs Become the Stars................... 112
Early Autumn Darkness, Livermore, Colorado.......... 114
Some Mornings... 115
This Hour 118
When I Wept the Animal 121
The Compassionate Darkness.................................... 122
Nocturne of the Western Night................................. 124
Lone Owl... 126

EIGHT
THE SOMNAMBULIST DREAMS
Dream in Which Frank Waters Is My Mother 129

NINE
LOSING MYSELF IN THE LARGER MEASURE OF NOW
Once, When We Were Alive...................................... 135
New Moon, October... 137
Thinking of Bai Juyi on Yet Another Day of Wind
  in Colorado 138
Back There in the Old Days 140

Ghost Town Train Stop on the "Old Prairie Dog Express"
   of the Burlington & Missouri River Railroad 142
Laramie Says 144
Lambing... 146
Return from Durango 147
If We Could Ask Water to Finally Forgive Water 151
What I Learned 153
The Rain That Doesn't Reach the Ground 154
The Barn at the End of the World 157

THROWING SALT AT MY MOTHER
Throwing Salt at My Mother..................................... 163

Notes 167
Acknowledgments 171
About the Author... 175

The Rain
That Doesn't
Reach the Ground

Virga is any form of precipitation that doesn't reach the ground. There could be rain virga or snow virga. But in either case, the precipitation evaporates somewhere on the journey from clouds toward earth.
  —*Weather Notebook,*
  Mount Washington Observatory

*Back where you lived, for those
who remember well, there will come
a glass face, invisible but still and real,
all night outside in the rain.*
  —William Stafford

TELL ME

Tell Me

Tell me again how the world came
to be. Hold the palm of my hand
in yours and read the tracings
of owls who flourished in moonlight,
even when the fog blurred
our seeing. Remind my body
scars that they were not always
with us. That sometimes the sun
was whole, and when we came West
we could name every tree. And bend
with the cottonwoods into the river.

Once, far back, the world said, *Listen.*
And we did. Now, when the wind calls
my name, I bow to its shadow and try
to forget the naming. Praying
that the wind *has* a shadow,
that the owls are there, allowing me
to dissolve. Calling
the moonlight. And not me.

ONE

THE WAY WEST

Beneath the Medicine Moon

When we came to Council Bluffs that winter,
the world seemed near. The low depth
of the Missouri in the cold
said what was inside us
had been frozen over, struggling all along.
In LeClaire, the day before, the docent
at the Buffalo Bill Museum had spoken
in low reverent tones about the Mississippi,
the flood plains and mosquito pools on its banks,
and the problem each spring
with the mischievous moorings of mayflies.

We had traveled as far as the sun
would allow. Sioux Falls. Cedar Rapids.
And south to the Colorado-Kansas border,
where a wanderer at the gas station told us tales
of grapefruit-sized hail the summer before
and the terrified bleating of lambs. We knew something
had to change, though we were unsure
what or how. The sky tilted toward us
as if listening from somewhere inside itself
it was sure we somehow knew.
We leaned forward into our past,
listening back hard. And then the moon rose,
golden, oozing a mixture of sunflowers
and kerosene, pouring out its insides
into us, through everything we thought
we saw. And heard. And wanted.
And, thus, believed we'd one day know
and begin to teach our learning to see.

The Way West

This is how it is in Livermore.
My wife wakes early in Colorado
summer to walk our beagle-hound
in the mountains before the heat. And the wind.
I stay up late writing, rattling my words
into the warmth of the kerosene lamp, urging the dark
parts of my life to slip away. Late mornings,
we absorb the coming clouds. We drink tea,
reminisce, map our future
breaths. Even argue a little about things
that don't matter. When afternoon comes
with its cruel hint of death's sickle, we hold
our breaths. And each other.
While shadows ride in through the kitchen
window and into the open places
in us from across the Laramie Plains.

The Western dead go by
outlaw names—cunning as Cole Younger
and Billy the Kid; bold as Frank and Jesse James;
heartbreakingly sad as the unsolved murder
of Belle Starr, the Bandit Queen—that try to name *us*
as horse thieves and robbers fleeing the sudden storm
of squealing train brakes. Boxcar doors
sliding open, unloading cavalry
and the pounding surprise
of hooves in dusty pursuit.

Evening comes on us, comforting yet cruel
with its dusky calm and animals we only glimpse
the shadows of. Yes, evening comes, warming us
like a good Greek shawl, woolen and fringed.
Moth-bitten yet whole. And I am amazed
these years long that my grandparents came all this way—
at least as far as Chicago, a Wild West to them
on the shores of Lake Michigan. That they left
their small island villages and crossed out the great water
that had told them *no*, somehow floating. Fearless.
Into a new world. Without gasping for breath,
or crying out into one another, or begging for a kerosene
lamp to hold the night away, to help the darkness
slip momentarily into an unpredictable dance
that promised to consume it.

Winter Almanac

Once, when we were young, we were very old.

    The wind went fierce, and books appeared

in the trees as if writing over and again the incessant

    need for love. In the black willows.

In the pines. We came to love, loving what the wind gave

    us. Time and again stood still, allowing our life,

hoping we'd catch on. And one plus one never again

    equaled zero. They left us—*numbers* left us—puzzled,

as we tried to learn to speak the bitter yet human

    salt. *Here—this story was given us—rub this salve*

into the wound, we were told by the trees, yet always

    in passive voice. Action stood dead before us,

though we tried to resuscitate it, mouthing the calming

    sound of now. We went West, knowing

the movement itself might find our finding. And *Colorado*

    became a word our bones grew into

along with Council Bluffs, Sharon Springs, and Ogallala.

    Each stop along our way was a manner of mouth.

And moths against the glass told us to turn off the lights,

    blow out the lamps. The wind went on being

the wind, fierce and full of itself, and the books it wrote

    told tales of old—woodchips, propane stoves,

and almanacs of grief. And how the people moved

    their lives here to there, charted by nomadic

stars. Or bees' blood gone wrong. How a kerosene lamp

    might finally be enough to prepare for weather,

especially those mornings moaning of wind and the bloated

    hours and habits of long-stubborn snow.

Train from Denver to Grand Junction

We looked through the glass
into the other world
where the years floated by without us.

A line of trees stood lost
in a murky rain
like souls departed
without the grief of a family
to bind them to Earth.

Part of the past was beginning
to blur. Someone asked the ticket taker
how long to Pueblo. And she said
something about lying down
on our back with wind in the mouth,
allowing it to depart through the left ear.

Green on the slopes from Denver
past Colorado Springs made us wonder
how much longer we could survive.
An ant crawling across the window
as we passed Pikes Peak far off to the south
was a hiker in Nepal searching for sherpas
in the Himalayas.

Without grief, the benevolent insects
seemed to die before the stinging ones.
Just as the good people we know crumble
when the light gets too heavy to hear.

The sun began to fall, and animals
emerged from the far trees.
And I had continued to age.
How could I have ever made it this far
for this long? How was my nocturnal self
to ever find balance among sunspots of sorrow?

The night whistle whirled through the Gunnison
River bottom, stirring fish and grit. Part of me
was sinking out there among the fin-flash
of trout in the shady shallows.

The trees seemed to be moving faster
and slower than the train. When would it stop,
I wondered, this sense that my two good feet
were not enough? And how might we make
the long night of our throats listen and not speak?

Drinking Tea in Mountain Moonlight, Trying to Think Only of Tea

When people talk too much, I once heard, they are bound to say the wrong thing.

*

Coyotes and hyenas have a lot in common. Both are wolves in wolves' clothing.

*

The wind is not so much the wind tonight but a ghost-voice the trees release into the air to convey the death of their breath no longer passing into people.

*

This tea is not so much a beverage but the blood-root of autumn sinking into itself the golden tips of the tea leaves.

*

We sip. We taste. We ache and mouth. Then there is no sound. Though our words are there. When the radio suddenly stops for a few seconds, then resumes, it must certainly mean our true love is thinking about the sudden death of the world.

*

Once, the word *once* got lost among a forest of numbers. Big numbers. Little numbers. And it became *Remember?* and *How About When?*

*

Say a man wears glasses. Say it is as if two fish eyes were peering back into the watery parts of his heart, swimming toward the dry banks of his brain.

*

You told me once that you loved me. I told you nothing is true except truth slowly unbuttoning its blouse to reveal riverous veins of moonlight.

*

Yes, the word *no* is smaller and oddly less definite than the word *maybe*.

*

There are many tales of mystery and imagination. For example, peer into the mirror.

*

Birds die too. We just rarely see the elaborate funerals ants hold for them.

*

If I die when I die, I would like you to tell me all about it, especially what light I will hear pulsing around me and not see.

*

I look at pools of moonlight hearing the wind. Yes, I mean the moonlight, the *moonlight* listening in. Then moments later, *I* hear the wind and crave the moon's slow milk. Pour more tea and hear the accordion breath of every day of pain. Unfolding. Bellowing in and out of me. Then I remember the old Zen master saying, *When you drink tea,* drink *tea.*

*

Now the moon pours down into the blotch marks of my bones. And I know that both the moon and my bones are bones in bones' clothing.

*

When you swallow the moon, the trees keep saying, swallow *the moon.*

*

There are many tales of mystery and imagination. For example, peer into the sad glance of your heart, which says, mis-says, and says again, *Everything I have ever sad somehow says through you.*

*

All these buffalo bones, the moon says, *are bison in people's clothing.*

*

Peer into the piles at your side. Say the depth of your sad just right.

*

Boil water. Steep tea. Absorb the agony of the leaves. Most doors lead nowhere unusual. Open one and jump through.

Hibernation

1.
Then came days of aching rain. The dirt
said, *Listen*. And what I heard was a wind
meant for the trees to feel each other
and see. I dreamed long, as if my dreaming
was awake. I dreamed an empty place
inside me full of fireflies I could see
then not. And the wind went on
and off. On and on. Forever.

My mother was there, or more precisely
her shadow. There was a horse munching wild
clover in the distance. It would not look up
no matter how loudly I called. Then my mother
was a she-wolf, a goldfinch,
then a whooping crane, and a great peace
came over me in the form of light, cooling rain.
And a calm moved upon me as if the wind
and I were lovers. As if rubbing against one another,
we created the whirl of the world. As if it were 7:39 p.m.
the entire morning and evening, beckoning the dusk.

2.
Now, both of my hands are full of wet earth.
And when I consider my life, I could use
a good cry, or better yet a fertile weeping.
Yes, I trust the earth. Enough, say,
to spell it three or four different ways
but always one that leads to the river.
Lightning is there and a vast darkness
we were not meant to see.

Yes, I am convinced you all love me,
or, at least, that you *believe* you do. This Western sky
betrays me moment by moment with mounting
cloud cover and gray. You would not want
my shadow to enter your day
and be part of the cave whose walls
you have chosen to draw upon with charcoal
to map the progress of your mouth
and save words for the family. The cave
you are certain is waiting
to preserve your winter rest, to cuddle
and cure the hurt of you.

Me. Mine. Moist. Exposed in the Medicine Bows

with a first line by Jack Spicer

Love to whatever is loved.

        Open like granite
      exposed in the Medicine Bows.

   1. For a long time, I've lived as an owl on fire in my chest
   2. Stars sink their thoroughly sunken into me

I am circling above you as if from below.

I am dissolved and dissolving and always turning
into my lockjaw self.

The cottonwood in the yard is homesick for the sycamore,
drawing last month's rain up out of hard ground.

Open a granite rock out on the Rawhide Flats.
Like medicine. Like thick and slow and home.

I do not pour out of myself.
Go to your room now and meditate.

On fire. An owl is on fire in my chest.

   1. Sincere and wind-driven quiet

2. Language that blurs and buries itself in the body like an osculant ox

Let a bird speak. Let me my talk and now (me, mine, moist).

Mostly, though, I hold a damp wound in my bone.
Wind drafts conjugating birds, current
lines of a poem, fierce and full of mending.

Pouring. I do not pour out of my mouth.
Nor you, from your left big toe.

The Western sky is somehow always east.
Colorado is both east and west of grief.

A bitterly blowing wind.
       I am aching for you wherever you go.

When Our Breath Overlaps with Ghosts

Then the wind stopped.
And in its place, the moon rose,
golden, crawling dusk out of the rabbitbrush
and brome. The dead are dead again,
and keep dying, luminous in the cheatgrass,
banked on the saddle northwest
between two ridges of Douglas firs. Wyoming
is close and far away at once.
As is its frontier past. And its mustangs pummeling
the plains all the way to Carson City
and Reno. My shadow, molded to this mountain,
outside chopping wood. A dazzling dead man has eyes
like a frozen postage stamp. Back in the specialty years
of airmail, we paid more to deliver our breath
across the continent, through the sky.
Now, the wind carries my silence
and its cure. The deer carcass I came upon
last evening on my gravel mountain
road somehow had my name on it, inscribed with salt.

Down the burly black water ridge,
the earth is slipping away. Each day. Each hour
of my life. I had wanted a brief respite from the clay
my body kept trying to convince me was my calling.
And the many sore places. The many sores
of my mouth kept repeating that I'd never find the word
I needed most. Tongue-stuck and stumped,
I was far away, and I was close.
I grew closer to myself even as I kept slipping away.

This is Colorado. This is now. Behind the moon
are sassafras stumps and teacups
from which I keep sipping,
trying to drain. The wild horses roughing the range
are wilder than the ominous thunderhead
in a cruel blue sky, the thunderclap
of their hooves telling me
I must go on. Reminding me that the turkey vultures
circling the house earlier this afternoon
fluffed their wingèd bleed, dazzlingly dervish
in their wind dance, ecstatic in their death offerings
as they cut my name into the sky
over and over again.

What the Moon Said

We dreamt the moon told us.
And what it said. And *how* it said.
It's hard leaving a place
you've always wanted to leave,
living two places at once.
Rows and rows of soybeans and corn.
And the floating ribs of gray barns
weathering, rising like beautiful boats
hazy on the horizon.

Carefully, I return to Indiana
and the woodsy scent of trees.
Sycamores. Elms. Shagbark hickories
peeling back the layers
like dreams that awaken, that awaken me,
then slowly deepen my sleep.

Colorado is everywhere
at once. Its junipers are now.

What the turkey vultures circling outside
my window this morning know
is something that scares my daylight.
Shags it away. Down into the culvert,
at the base of the gravel
drive, tightening my veins
so the blood vessels
of the world contract.

There is an underground river beneath this
arid land telling me, *The layers, peel back the layers here.*
When I go places, I go. What I leave
behind are decades of woods
that have worked themselves into me—
sassafras, wormwood, pawpaw, and oak.
What I leave are acres of droning
flat, achings of mosquitoes, flesh flies,
and crowded clouds. And the floating ribs
of the beckoning barns of Indiana,
blowing in and out, expanding and contracting
in cornfield wind with a breath
seemingly broken
yet whole.

Driving Across the Great Plains

And each small town. Each small town
keeps crawling me back, carving itself
through itself. Cutting into the Indiana tree bark
of my bones as a supposed way home.
Say I call out every day, by God, to myself.
Say I'm lost like the sound of gravel
in the shallows. Say I am the texture of wind
in the mouth, slowly easing out
back unto the world. The sun. The sun comes up
across these plains. The moon bleeds back the night.
Flakes of snow keep saying *Colorado*,
even as I pass—miles and miles east—
Nebraska towns like Sidney and Broken Bow.

I've called. Called out to the dead.
I've called and combed my voice
over and again through the buffalo
grass. Rolled it, mud-blotched, into the river bottom
where all things are beautifully said. Sad.
Where the wind goes slack in evening
lanterns lit by moths. I didn't feel
things. Didn't feel the earth
for a long time. Still, I kept driving west,
past Ogallala and Julesburg, telling myself
the mountains would surely stop me.
And I felt whinges of wind, both behind me
and before, mimicking me as I clenched
with each breath I took to reassure myself
I had done my best. That I had done

all I possibly could. That the cottonwoods
each autumn fed the North Platte
bags of their brilliant gold. That the land I was eating
was eating *me* with each mile
I pursued, each leaf somehow falling
into me and through.

Only the Wind

*He loved warm winter days when woodlands opened
their summer secrets to a passerby.*
    —Jim Wayne Miller

Remember the bridge over the Maumee?
The woods swallowed it one night. It grew dark
and darker still. And our fear fattened on what lay ahead.
Now, when the wind rustles the wild mountain grass
outside my window, I imagine days waiting for me
when I will no longer be. Only the wind
will be here, and a few snakes and mice.
Beetles and ants will go on
climbing the Mummy Range
of the leafy stems, causing
the grass to bow a little
with their weight
and effort at the top.
Everything will love everything else.
The world will go on being reverent to the world.
And it will surely not miss me—
that insignificant impression
my body bent into wind—
and will eat itself clean
without me, not even remembering I ever walked
this path or left threads of myself behind,
clawed at by cockleburs that tried to hold me.

Grasshopper and Cricket

1.
Let's call the world all kinds of things. Let's weep
the animals. Weep them through our blood.
Let's press the primordial pulse.
Measure the changing weather
of our mouths. Walk through fog
as a way of seeing our insides
blur. Drive through rain,
north, to Tie Siding, to Casper,
to visit the pioneer dead,
a day when they remain alone
and are mournfully moist.
Sip the darkness of an hour. Soak up mountain midnight
snow so the daylight hidden inside each flake
guides the night like lanterns on prows of ships
that help us plow the dark.

2.
So much for how we hope for light.
So much for the lilting lanterns of the world.
Sometimes it's simply a word that guides us through.
Is it *puppy* or *pup*? A *hound dog* or a *hound*?

Words stick in the throat,
startle us in the long way down.

My beagle pup is fascinated with beetles,
moths, and especially grasshoppers.

Anything that jumps, darts, and dazzles.
We step out through burnt July
cheatgrass, from which newly hatched
grasshoppers leap out of nowhere, seemingly
out of themselves. They taunt this puppy, barely a year old,
who is seeing things as if for the first time.
She pounces, leaps after them, clumsy as she learns
to inhabit her body. Blaisie, almost a grasshopper
herself.

    I say, *Leave the cricket alone,
"Blaze." It's just a baby. Like you.*
Then catch myself doing it yet again,
that weird reversal of grasshopper
and cricket, though I know better,
know as much as the wind pouring down
from Laramie. Lightning in the distance
over Cheyenne, its electrical tug threatening
the horizon, though far enough away for calm.
Virga in the clouds streaking dark gray—that rain
that never reaches the ground. That rain
whose swaggering sweep keeps eluding me.

3.
Let's call the world, *the World*. Let's call the rain
what it is. Is it rain not raining that I see
or cricket-scratch in wind? Lightning, say,
or my insides trying to ignite? Grasshopper
twitch or puppy brain pouncing
on anything that moves?

I walk our dirt road, late most nights below spraying
stars and milky moon. Sometimes a yowling
in the distance. Mountain lion, bobcat, or lynx?
I say *bobcat*, hoping for the best.
Mary Ann, concerned with my nightly walks,
calls it *mountain lion reported up from the Poudre*,
hoping to startle my brain
awake.

        And so the wind comes as wind.
Rain, when it comes, as rain. My pup as perfectly pure
and curious pup—not grasshopper- or cricket-bliss. My own
puppy brain finally absorbing midnight
moves of *mountain lion* with a silent stalking
that now has me walking earlier with the sun.

4.
Let's call the world all kinds of animals.
Let's attend to the bent of our blood.
Let's pursue the primordial pulse.
Let's menace our mouths, invite the changing weather
inside. Call the daytime dark,
the night a slip of blistering sun.
The crickets and knotty pine walls of our past
as the grasshoppers and propane tanks of now.

Somewhere, far back in my sleep, I feel the tongue-
stuck and the lame:

    Leave the cricket alone,
    "Blaze." It's just a baby. Like you.

That weird reversal of grasshopper
and cricket—always there—like the lift and dip
of the mountains that sometimes *rise*
and sometimes *fall*, the Mummy Range
which, named for the dead,
seems so much alive. Settling the dark
in the dark, like a ship
anchored on the horizon.

Is it a *ship* out there in the drifting night
or simply a *boat*? A *mountain*, say, or *hill upon hill*?
Is it rain not raining that I see or cricket-scratch in wind?
My name beginning to lapse
and blur, or my breath
smothered in stars, known only
as *Wind, Lightning,* or *Rain*?

Or my childhood mouth, rubbed
and raw, known only as *Cricket*,
absent in this burnt July
                  grasshopper haven?

If I would but call my puppy, *pup*?
If I would but dub Blaisie, *Blaze*?

      If I would but call the world,   *the World.*

Call the rain, *snow*. And the sleet—   severe
            in my mouth—
                      shame.

Call the world what it *is* and *isn't*.

And as I grow and old and come to know—

                                      sing it so.

TWO
THE SOMNAMBULIST DREAMS

Dream in Which Georgia O'Keeffe
Is My Father

This is the way to hold the axe, she said. *And bring both arms down together to split the wood.* Somehow, Georgia O'Keeffe was with me in Indiana, in the backyard woods in which I had grown up, instructing me on how to be a man. *Remember, you are part of the woods*, she told me. *And when you chop wood you are also cutting into your own core.* Then she reached into me and grabbed my hand, and we were watching the clouds from my kitchen window in Livermore, Colorado. Her paintings surrounded us, on each wall that did not house a window. I knew I was supposed to stare, to peer through them into the other world. *I could be a cloud*, I thought, silently of course. Yet she heard me. Georgia O'Keeffe heard me, telling me to stay grounded, to take to the forest and kiss each aspen tree I came upon. *It's the only gift I can give you, father to son*, she said. And I knew she was right. That somehow I had been thrown from the loins of Georgia O'Keeffe into a pelvis of sky. That she was here to teach me the words of the Indiana woods. The Colorado forest. Words and phrases like *walk* and *see* and *merge your mind with the bears denning down by the Elkhorn. And the throat*, she chided. *Don't forget the ruby in the hummingbird's throat.*

There was so much red in her words. Blood words. Sunset words. The moon-rising-over-the-Western-plains words. Words that held no bruise. I told her that I loved her early paintings too, the less famous ones, the ones from back East in which she'd painted me as more than one barn handling dark the coming storms. And she smiled that Georgia O'Keeffe smile, leaning against a doorway in Abiquiú, far away from me, yet close, like many fathers few of words. Fathers who take to the desert to teach the lost language of trees. Who dream of clouds and become a cloud. And I knew she was mine forever, in the electrical pulse tugging at me. In me. Calling my bones back into the primordial pose of a ram's head floating above hills with a hollyhock where I knew I could live with her forever in both the bone *and* the bud. Father to son, until I birthed my own nest of sparrows to teach me the interweavings of both worlds at once. The father and the son, the woman and the man, the animal and its bloom—each twig bent and circled into a nest, torn yet whole. Each desert grain of sand I was floating above, longing to become.

THREE

SOMETHING AKIN TO KIND BLOODLIGHT

Dead Grouse

Of course I thought of Jim Harrison
With his bird dogs decades in Michigan and Montana
How this bird fell from the sky
And why
This dead grouse in the driveway
Suddenly upon me in my midnight flash-lit path
Lying in gravel
Like shot dead by the stars
Her little body
Her perfect mottled bird body
Already falling into the earth
Already sinking away
Like words of love
Like so many words of touch and hurt
How many times did she fly over our home
Wondering at the human commotion
Below?
I look long into her speckled breast
So much breath had broken into each day and night
Into the break of evening's dusk before the coming dark
And what would swallow her
So much flight
She knew she could only glide so long
She could not pursue
Herself to this final spot
This mix of gift and grit
This is not Livingston, Montana, or even northern Michigan
There is nothing *living* here at this moment
Even here in *Live*rmore, Colorado, among cheatgrass and pines
But the midnight sky spitting at us both

As I peer into what she spent her life trying to avoid
And spent her motherhood teaching her chicks to shun
Such a small powerful bird in my path
The Dusky Grouse of the Rockies
Unusual on the ground
Like fierce inverted weather
Like weather reversed
Among the echo of footfalls
My footfalls
I am used to looking up into her
Underbelly of stars
Into her
Thrumming
Her otherwise beauty but am left now touching
My chest in reverence and leaving her here
Bathed in starlight
As is my hope for her
To fly one final time
Into the depth
Of darkness and the bodies of the fox family
With three ravenous kits
Denning on the hill behind us
Whining for a good death
To give them life

Prayer to the Red Fox Who Appeared Near the August Blue Moon, 2023

Like you, I've looked for answers in fox tracks.
—Eric Pankey

Walking dusk along this mountain
road—the moon bloated, two days
from full—I felt an inexplicable urge
to turn and walk the other way.
And there she was, a red fox,
not more than twenty yards
before me, which had been behind.
Her tail fluffed and full.
She had emerged from out of the rabbitbrush,
the cheatgrass, thinking I had passed.
I stopped. *She* stopped. Quail flutter
in my throat. We stared into one another
and through. The long years
for which we had both longed
hung there between us.

I touched my chest, rubbing my palm
in prayer across it, over my heart. And again.
More deeply. I wanted to bow before her,
bend and kneel, take the dusk's
dust, carve the gravel of this mountain road
deep into my bones.

I wish my life. I wish parts gone—
all the tearing apart. The terrible, the torn.
I wish I could have taken in her

delicacy—her shedding, her rust.
The way she paused, lifted a paw,
and looked long into me. Taken her
forepaws into my palms
and kissed them, tenderly,
over and over. Over and again.
Through the cavernous depth of the dark,
the deepening dark of *my* dark,
until the moon blistered me
with its cold breach of snow, crawling forth
my shadow. The moon emptying
me as it bent back the night
and went fully. Full.

At the Pawnee National Grasslands

Colorado Eastern Plains

The only sound out here
    is wind pouring through wind.

This is where the sun and moon
    scrape into one another and blur.

The Chalk Bluffs. Buttes seemingly rise
    out of their own stone coffins.

Mice bone cracks
    the mouths of owls.

The world of the dead collides
    with the world of the dead.

Hammerblows of wind pummel the dusk,
    batter the buffeting at my feet.

The buffalo grass keeps bending
    toward me, plowing, pleading,

knowing it must go on, certain it will
    one day get in. Get into me and through.

Coyote Crossing the Road

She is too young to be young. She moves
as if the first season, exacting her stance.
This is home because some animals die.
She came to alter my skin with her breathing.
This crude wind. Somewhere in the scaling knife
we call life. More dog than wolf, more wolf
than the mange she manages to avoid.
Ask your skin how and why it aches.
I once wrote Woolrich, angry, because
their parka hoods were trimmed with coyote ruff.
So much of us is covered in the obliteration
of others. Ask your skin. Ache it. Ask it
and ache of it as if. As if alive,
willows moan when I step onto blades
of buffalo grass. We don't know the weight
of things. We can't measure pounds of her fur
because her coat weighs different when dead.
Some things we say. Some we safe away
in a pile of dried bones. With nineteen
recognized subspecies, the coyote
is many animals at once. She crosses
a road. We glimpse of her and ache. The distance
between words. Worlds. Now she blends into and with.
She is too old to be old. She is the proper need,
an immediate wind, shadow blessings
of nineteen probable names we can't know
the weight of. She slurries my path, glances back
by not looking, hiding in the rabbitbrush. I want
to ask if willows moan. If the buffalo

grass bends. I know this moment's depth,
that I will never see her pelage again.
Her gentle step steps into me and through.
Such a fleeting moment on the road.
She came to alter my skin. And she is there
now inside the insides of things
rolling in mud, biting a paw, standing
on the ridge of my breathing
skin as good long animal luck.

Lamenting the Full Golden Moon
Two Weeks Before It Breaks Itself in Two

August Blue Moon, Livermore, Colorado, 2023

Bobcat face
golden brown
looking
     down
onto me,   *into* me,
seeming so
          comfortable
about to cut itself,
       chew itself,   loose,
pawing then
    clawing
its permeable   human
perch,
digging further
    into   me,
into everything I know
    and *think*   I know,
and all I want
to want
to become is
     settled there
tearing my
insides   in and   out
  in   and out
of themselves,
shredding them   and the sun
hidden therein
      apart

Passing a Field of Antelope on Colorado County Road 74E, Pondering the Darkness

1.
Before dark, near the border
of dusky animal light,
this touch. This
touch of primordial dark.
I suddenly absorb it, see on the county road home
eight, maybe nine, antelope
in the field to my left.

These pronghorn are grazing lazily
as if they are not poised on the edge
of the world. As if the rain in their bellies
is not fire on a ridge or volcanic lapses
of snow. As if dreams themselves
are not already asleep, dangling
from a ridgetop on a spur. As if the dreams
of the unprotected are not blurring
with the dreams of the despaired.

2.
In Wichita, Kansas, my friend's
father is trying to hang onto his earlier life,
grasping a CD
of his son's favorite music,
allowing the sound of his thinning
years to reshape memory,

to secure a thread
from his navel back to his son
and to his son's mother
and to his *own* mother before her.
The cottonwoods bow and bend
all the way to Galva
like elders
protecting their young,
and the Hungarian Grouse lift the darkness
of the field with them into who knows where,
though it be toward the light
that gives the grass a luminous shape,
even when it darkens down
into autumn.

3.
The antelope graze
as if each shrinking shred
of light in the buffalo grass
was meant only for them. As if each shred
came unto this field solely to nourish the swathes of white fur
on their underbellies and rumps, and on the underbellies
and rumps of their young. What touches them,
touches us. Their little horns
protruding from their sturdy pronghorn heads
like partially formed spears
too stunted to stab the grass
but pointing the way down
into layer upon layer of light.

4.
Lord help them. Lord help
the fire ants clinging to the underside
of an elm leaf. Lord
help us all. Keep us human.
Keep us most human
even amidst explosions
of sorrow. Where our sadness grows
by degrees in relation to the rain.
There is a stirring across the field,
past the lolling antelope
who curious the grass
with new and wordless ways of eating.
A stirring that promises weeks
of whiteout conditions
and a blurring of ever-blowing snow
that will allow us to absorb the fog and cold
and warm them before the iron stoves of Colorado.

5.
The wind touches us. The air
touches us. The sun. The moon
and its oozing pools. This touch,
this touch we wrestle down
into the base of things
where the dead crow
and the ants burgeoning
its half-eaten belly seep into the soil
and somehow drench the roots
of a shagbark hickory
and allow its peeling

layers to reveal depths
of aging—the many wrongs and weathers
of the world—welcoming a sky
full of terrified birds
that perch and blather back
the brutal dark,
the ageless achings of the wind.

Brain-Tanning the Hides

*first anniversary of the 2012 Colorado High Park Fire
that took our first mountain home and many homes of
our neighbors*

All that separates us from *us*. The ripping apart from here
to there. How tanned. How tender. A solution of animal brains
to break down the hide, smooth away the holes.

When we sleep with and unto and through our own skin.
How soft we become when we have slept the animal.
Like the Blackfeet, we must remove the brains from the elk,

wrap them in the hide thirty perfect days. Soak them
in urine. Loosen the fibers. Unhair the hide
with a knife. We should similarly brain-tan our own selves?

The skins are dried stiff. Dirty with soil and gore.
Blossoms feeling far back past possibility to ash?
How can it possibly be 365 days of loss? Of rebuilding?

Someone lost five elk hides in our fire. Grief-bruised dust
of the heart. A Wyoming sky just north of us is falling
down a draw. Sighing into the mad mudflats of the Sinks.

One neighbor recovers from forty-nine weeks of strain.
Another struggles with the doctors' dour sense
of time. Alkaline. Pungent. We somehow go on.

A kerosene lantern the color of pheasant blood holds

tonight's full moon close to Earth. A moon so close
we can hear the scraping. Can almost hear it tan *any* hide

and soften the animal's heart, long since removed.

Time Was

This winter they'll call me *Snow Geese Over Dry Land*.
    They'll say they told me so, that the idea
of reincarnation is a ruse, that you only live once

and should grab the most from fin and feather.
    They'll tell me over and again that winter
is not a state of mind. That if I want to be warm

I should not try to think myself warm
    but should move south to Phoenix or Baja.
Time was when I could drive my car

the eleven miles home up the Livermore Valley
    Road and not be told how to think.
That the coyote crossing in front of me was there

to quiet my mind, drop the voices of the day's dread,
    and reinforce the wild ways I see, that the dead
raccoon at the roadside was not a bad omen but a fortuitous

force of fur. So, this winter they keep calling me
    many hurtful things, from *Snow Goose
Afoot*, to *Fox Face in Dirt*, to *Dirty Fingernail*

of a Wobbling Moon. I've learned to listen and deepen
    their ways of speak. To misplace my words,
if I must, and delve into how to be and not be

myself. To pray to the golden eagle circling
    my home to bless me with its wing-snap
of death. To carry the worst of me away.

Everything We'd Wanted to Say

When I lived before,　　　　rain was the only season.
We returned to that weather　　　　　　　　to see
if our lives could be　　　　elongated,　　　even a little.
You'd want me　　　　to be truthful, right?　To speak,
even when wet?　　　　　　Even if I don't believe
　　　　　　entirely in people, I know
the animals I have wept　　　　and those　　who weep
me. And　　　　*for* me. Birds　　　　dominated the sky,
coming as if from our mouths,　　　though we were silent
children. I mean,　　　　*We were silent children*,
not, *We were silent,*　　*children.* I'd never call anyone
or thing a child　　　　　　　without their permission,
with or without　　　　the comma's pearl.

We lived by permission.　　　　　By what we allowed
to sound.　　　　　What the world allowed
was always clear,　　　even if not　　　　　spoken.
But the wood-burning stove　　　　heated us well
and burned more　　　than cedar　　　　　and oak.
Parts of ourselves　　　flew out of our mouths, like birds
　　　　　manic and mute　　　　into the intelligent flames.
I cried for each word,　　　singed, shrouded, and bound.
Everything we'd wanted to say　　　　　　　to the world
got said—but only into the stove,　　　lodged there
　　　　　　behind the iron door.

Now I careful   when I speak. I even
    intentionally skip   a word now and then.
The gaps   seem to mark   the emptiness
that needs to be filled.   And the animals.
They are always there   to help. Even the dead
raccoon at the side of the road   as we drove down
the mountain   this afternoon for friends
and conversation.   Poor thing was smashed,
road-bitten, as if grasping   for its soft birth,
for the mothering   mud. As if dreaming
a backwoods swamp it thought   it could wallow in
the long winter long. As if   it had dragged itself from as far
as Indiana   just to remind me my life.

Look at the sun,   I told my wife
as we drove past   its remains and observed a stirring
of silence.   *It's slanting   through the long struggle
of the animal's throat   as if aching
to   speak, to   say   something
whole, moon-   bitten,   to us,   but only
indirectly.*   And then I thought through   the very quiet
of my skin—less clearly and much   garbled   from the road:
*It keeps asking us   to read the meaning   of sudden sun
splotches in the cattails   and golden yellow   flower heads
of the rabbitbrush.   But mostly in sun   circles
          beckoning us from blotches   of fur
          we have carried long inside us
and from the sun gauze—   soaked and   soggy—
          of the bloodstained road.*

Spoken Into

This could be Dakota, the entire way
to the night sky. In our little cove
of a dream, the stars—anchored inside
our mouths—keep saying, *water, water, wind, and fire.*
Where was the earth we'd tried so long?
The ground we thought we'd walked on?
We had lost it some midnights
among the startling days
as the shade grew heavy, holding our names
wobbling but seemingly intact.

My grandmother could bake blackberry pie
to rival the dusk, a darkness whose simple grace
was to lie down at the close of each day, inside
us, to calm us like the beagle-hound had,
head thrust out in front on its paws. The moon
went on being the moon even when
the maples strained red
beneath it. Even when pines cut
woodblocks of Japanese bonsai
deeply into it.

Now, years late, this is Colorado, though it could
just as easily be the Missouri Breaks, Cedar Falls,
or even Claxton Mills. The stars in our mouths
make strange moth movements, fluttering
upon our tongues as if what we speak
is the depth of light we need
to get to. And the trying, hard, to get there.

But the stars, in space, also call forth
the shade—those dark places we finger
tenderly when we think no one is looking.
As if calling the blood. As if calling back
from the bruised walls of caves
where bears den-up for winter, fat
from blackberry brambles and trout.

How to account for each finger
and what it feels? How to calm
the remaining pines carving the moon
into simple, discernible chunks?
Each cut, a slice of what we know
we had once been and what we hope
we can again one day become.
The way we long for primordial wool.
Put on a shirt. Adjust a button.
And lie with the night sky that lays down
its scars into the galaxies we glimpse
of and weep.

More Palomino, Please

for Marilyn Krysl, 1942–2024, author of
More Palomino, Please, More Fuchsia

The wind, the wind, the terrible wind. Coming from the Flatirons tonight, Marilyn.

Golden horses with white manes and swishing tails have pummeled down.

More this, you say.

Had this been your belovèd Kolkata and not Boulder, crows would have circled you, quarreling over your tongue, throat, your Bay-of-Bengal blue eyes. Had this been the Ganges River, your ash would have fallen far into the centuries' depths.

But you are here, now, in both the Colorado buffalo grass and canyon walls at once.

You are flying into your own death as if death does not exist.

You are stepping into it beyond the wing-beat of age.

You are alone as you fly further into yourself, into everything.

More that, you tell us, opening a hole
from the cottonwood's sorrow into its soul.

The horses along Highway 36 west into Boulder are browsing the ground, noses buried in grass hocks-high, as if in continuously grazing they will keep the world calm. They do

not seem to notice how horses on the western ridge have
soothed the sky into a palomino-gold-cream.

Have turned the tone of your bones gold.

Just another sunset in your gorgeous poet's throat moving off
into the bloodsmoke of your years among us?

Another day in the life of death?

Down the canyon the horses pour. Appaloosas, pintos,
chestnuts, and roans.

The world could never tame you, Marilyn. The color of death
never consume. You, the unbridled bride of nouns.

Now, you are gliding away on thick clouds pastured there.
Clouds the texture of clay, silt, and wind-blown grass.

> *More this*, you say. *More that.*

You are galloping—golden and white—into the tone of your
poems, full of horse-heart sorrow. The unfettered resting place
of a voice that called down stars into itself—so you could see
enough to weep words back into healings that ease yet hurt.

Where are my palominos, you ask, *with their magnificent manes?*
Give me palomino, more palomino, you insist, as you soar
further from us yet remain, folding into the golden rose of
your still-singing throat.

> *More fuchsia. Please,* you say, bounding into the sky,
> pounding the calm ground of the horizon.

Driving All Night from Here to There Is Sometimes Nowhere at All

Trucks on Highway 40
are passing through Steamboat Springs
during my two a.m. walk as if they are night
watchmen on an ocean freighter.
The rumble of tires and groan
of brakes awaken the shadowy creases
of night we fold ourselves into.
But the red trailer lights of the big rigs
keep penetrating the impenetrable dark
with something akin to kind bloodlight.

The water of the night is deep. The water
is always so deep it stirs
the dented depths. We fall so far into
ourselves we are often lost
among mammoth wings of manta rays
and the mud pulse of moray eels.

Where are they going, and where
have they been? I imagine loading
docks, double shifts, and fluorescent lights
taking on their load. They must surely be going
over Buffalo Pass, or perhaps Rabbit Ears,
then on through the night sprawl
of ranches and the 597 dreams
of the 597 residents in the wide river valley of Walden,
and up into Laramie or Cheyenne. How much further
will they travel, and through what
waters, to search for themselves?

And where have I been? Why tonight,
walking this path in this otherwise quiet mountain
town, am I leaving the inheritance
of stars to float among the working dead?
I remember similar crossings
from this person to that, from what I had hoped
to say and didn't, loading, unloading
myself, as if leading the best parts
away to Medicine Bow, Chugwater, or Sheridan.

The moon keeps pouring through
the headlamps of the traveling
dark, telling the road *no, maybe,* or *more.*
Highway 40 keeps calling, crawling,
and absorbing, dissolving into me
the moon and its brood.
And the beautifully brutal
bloodlights of the big rigs,
brighter now, awakening
with their brakes, somehow
keep reflecting the starts and stops
of my past—and all my night
shifts of oceans, years,
and the persistent stripping of gears.

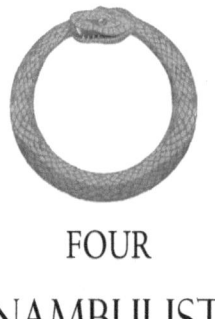

FOUR

THE SOMNAMBULIST DREAMS

Dream in Which Cormac McCarthy Dreams He is Dreaming Me Dreaming Him

He woke. I woke. We both slept into one another and through.

    He sat the horse. I buffed the saddle, grasped

the cantle. He insisted the animals had died. I wept them

    in my blood. He crossed the border into Mexico.

I journeyed north into the intimate vasts

    of the far territories, the ancient boreal forests

and primeval plains. Somehow, east was west. Snow was rain.

    Clouds pierced the sun. Trees heaved in the wind.

We were sitting cross-leggèd *inside* the trees yet climbing

    limb by limb the rough outer bark. A coyote howled

all the way from Colorado. She was an owl screeching through

    me. Throughout the night. Cormac McCarthy turned

in his sleep. And my throat went terribly dry. Parched. Sad.

    All the animals were alive even when dead.

He stood the night as I lay dreaming of him dreaming

me. The wet earth was quiet, still, and motionless

as it churned through me. Cormac was silent, calling

my name. And I heard myself crying out,

stunned. My tongue stuck with studs. Caught in iron combs.

He woke. I woke. And we slept as if the blood-root

we were was a river rustling to Santa Fe. Quietly awake.

FIVE

THE UNFORGIVING WAILING OF THE WIND-DRENCHED WIND

A Theory of Taxidermy

*after an evening in the saloon of The Grand
Hotel, founded in 1890, Big Timber, Montana*

Water was so deep we ate bread.
The bar was full of dead animals
with proud contented gaze. The bullet
or the bow brought peace? Not on your life,
but on theirs, as Montana trains exchanged
couplings out back for coal. Winter was hard.
Chickens scratched the grass, pecked their own eggs
open as if trying to grasp the essence
of their own ass. That's the way it is sometimes.
You stare at a map of Chicago
and pray that the tape on the wall won't stick.
French paint is the last thing you need
when scouring your lower intestine
with a candle. It would be easier
to imagine feeding a sparrow gin
and directing its beak with your left hand
in slow ovals over your desk.
Where is the window, and how might you bleed?
How might you carve an egg of light
as a way out? How might a simple apple
of glass become a bullet hole
intended for public display, for allayed
squawks and alleged snorts above the booth?
Geese frozen in flight, bighorn sheep sizing
both you and your conspicuous coffee up.
That enormous elk on the juke box wall

old as the only lodge in town that took its name.
The Santa Fe is surely not transporting hay
to Butte. Winter grass was hard as chicken scratch
on gold plaques, trophy printing far too easy to read.
Everywhere, dead animals on the heavenly wall
had the look of knowing what stood
behind brown vacant glass. Eyes shot inward
like a Monet lily swallowing a bridge,
like frightened eggs at the spring pleading.

Drinking Coffee at the Only Bar in Dixon Because Richard Hugo, James Welch, and J. D. Reed Had Whiskey There

You have ached taking your aches up the hill.
—Richard Hugo

The mountains come in ten stiff syllables
like shot glasses uneven on the bar.
The river staggers past town, having drunk
itself drunk in the winding way here.
Everyone's lung is bitter in Dixon.
No one wanted to lose it but had to. Sure,
we smoked, but the mills killed it faster.
We have ached as if aching was enough.
If you ask me my name I'll hide in lakes.
Sometimes there is pain we simply can't say.
Tomorrow is too much like yesterday. If I say
I hurt, believe me I hurt. Scald the coffee.
Bring me a second cup. Cutthroat trout
and deep streams come to calm me. The days
keep blurring right out of themselves.
I can't seem to say anything just right. Still,
I won't give up this barstool of words
or the bighorn sheep eyeing me from the wall.
If I could, I'd die while writing a poem.

Big Timber, 1998

Suddenly, it was Montana. Thirty-five degrees
in June. Sleet like hawk-claw through denim
shirts lined with red flannel. North Dakota
wind still pressing like a hive. Those hitchhikers
we left in a blur back in Bismark,
a part of ourselves we'd rather forget.

And each town had a name. Even those marked
No Services. A name that made them stand stark as lepers.
Someone touched a wound. The sore was always
open. *Did you remember the hats? Indiana
water for the dog? Her treats? That sharp smelling
spice to make curry with at the cabin?*
Were what we remembered and forgot really
indicators of love, or just how
the rain and wind shaped our lives?

And every name had a town. Big names
like *Bridger* and *Bozeman*. Little names
like *Thurlow*, *Hysham*, and *Vananda*
that seemed larger, almost diamond-glow,
when cut by slanting sleet. We focused
on our beagle-hound and wondered what
her thirst meant for us, how her sudden yelps
at Pompeys Pillar might say the climb
along cold wet boards was worth it.

How could he have carved his name fourteen feet
high in 1806? Something is always eroding.

It's not just the Yellowstone whingeing through
the willows, opening at rimrock for ghosts
of buffalo still pleading loudly with William Clark.
He wrote in his journal that the bellowing kept his men
awake throughout the night and disturbed
their almost-dreams with wallow dust and dirt.

What was attempting to sound from bullboat
and rut? From blotches of snow
browning on tattered buffalo hide?
From bee-weave like spun sugar in sagebrush?
Our beagle seemed to know. Snorting like a vacuum
over 1968 shag, she made the damp
boardwalk part of that sleep that came
later that night as satisfied paw twitching
and high-pitched, submarine-sound pleasure yelps.

We found the cabin in Big Timber beneath twilight
shadow-cloud covering the lot like a wet tongue
over a still-damp calf. A thick herd
with a baby white buffalo framed
and restless in Red River wind
lodged over the rocker.

                        We set out the candles.
Brewed tea. Discussed the cost to the county
of copper and coal. We sat on the sofa
with the beagle on an afghan between us,
holding hands and somehow feeling young
love trailing our first nineteen years together
from Indiana to Montana, past the smoke
of teepees and open ghosts,

the incessant sandpaper wind from Bismark
grinding rimrock and grunting its name
across sunglint shale in the Yellowstone shallows.

We savored our tea, absorbed the darkness,
counted our miles to arrive, and saw through
the window, in the distance, over dune-like plains,
train cars passing like a row of slouching
black camels—coal-smudged and slow—
steady, Bactrian, tattered-tail-to-tired-jaw.
Hide-blotched and purposeful Silk Road steps.

Graves at Victor

> *When Teddy Roosevelt traveled to the Mining
> District near Victor, via the Short Line (the Colorado
> Springs & Cripple Creek Railroad), he exclaimed,
> "This is the ride that bankrupts the English
> language."*

1.
They needed somewhere to lay the dead
following the fire of 1899. A pine shack in the alley
behind Jennie Thompson's Dance Hall
was to blame for the flames. *All that brothel heat,*
they said, *needed somewhere to go.* The lower slopes
of Battle Mountain still look
like they're at war, as if morning
coffee could never sizzle-calm
the bacon. Even the possibility
of over-easy eggs smothering down the plate.
They needed somewhere to lay
the miners and their families, well before
the spark. Hard hats and stifled living
meant a high chest of dirt.
The unmarked graves hurt worse.
White crosses never mean white.
Say, *Anything is nothing.* Repeat,
There is no sun at Sunnyside Cemetery.
We came with the rain, and the rain
will drag us home three and a half hours north
to Livermore, the tough of this town stuck
in our tongue, mining tipples tentative

as toothpicks toppling, stark with rust.
Teddy Roosevelt was wrong.
This is not the view *that bankrupts
the English language*. That view now
is nothing but mine tailings and dirt.

2.
I won't say it's not a pretty place,
this cemetery hill.
I won't say it doesn't hurt.
I walk among the names of the dead,
holding them one by one on my tongue.
Ella Porter and I must surely
have been in love, at least ten
or eleven of her thirty-seven years.
Even though we'd never met. Even as I scowl
down the weight of her gray-stone now,
the afternoon wet blurring away her years.
And Minnie Denson. With a name like that
she surely must have been beautiful,
dancing privately with her man
one night in a kitchen that smelled of salt pork
and blackened beans. Kerosene came and went
through the dark of the dead.
As did the gold, firing their lives
as they learned to love themselves
and feel whole in the thick animal night.

3.
Fragments of lives. Fragments
of some lives are here. They gather
in this cemetery like magnet filings
pointing north. Gather in my chest.
My words are wrong. Biscuits and gravy
this morning at the Fortune Club bludgeoned me
with breakfast chatter from Ginny,
the server from Georgia, who left
thirty years before only to complain now
upon her return about the new mining gloom.
What do we absorb eating in a place
that used to be a brothel? Desire, boredom, pleasure
unfulfilled? So much for toast sopped
in egg yolk. So much of the air remains
intact, *in* my lung and out,
like moments of touch we recall
in this limb and that. Like the unconscious
twitching of a finger that keeps gesturing
who knows where.

4.
Surely, I too would have looked for love
in a kitchen kerosene lamp, kicking
the town over into smolder
and smoke. I have done far too much time
and not enough, nudging away the day.
And my mistakes. Make no mistake—
they moan so loud they menace the dead.
Yes, the dead here are dead.
Even ghosts in the historic Victor Hotel

don't bother with me. I'm too far
along, and I'm too far gone.
I don't have a name in Victor but wish
it were *Eustis* or *Colton* or Ella's quiet plea
of, *Darling, Kiss the Rain
Right Out of My Heart*. There's nothing
victorious in Victor. The cemetery's
in sections as if the dead
can't reckon. The *Elks at Rest*
have missed the spring rut. And the sign
as you enter town—*Population 500
and 623 Dogs*—fails to count
each drop of rain grazing Ella's
grave, or Minnie's, or Ona's stone.
Or even the air Jennie Thompson
and her women breathed, making me
love them—each *one* of them—
and the hard of their lives even more now
in the ride that brought me
here to this most gorgeous of views,
this bankrupt place.

The Death of Nikola Tesla

When Nikola Tesla died, a little light eased out of his left ear. Sparrows pulled apart from his dead belly to reveal nomadic paths of bees, alight with the northern lights repeating themselves on journeys from Namibia to Brazil. Telegrams poured in from the four corners of grief. Buffalo Bill proclaimed from his grave that this is what happens when you kill the cow before the bull. Others from beyond also mourned: César Vallejo copied *Tesla* over and again into the skin of five notebooks, in the script of three different hands; Admiral Peary and roustabout Cook said the feud was finally over, that there never really *was* a North Pole to dispute anyway; and Edison wept near his recorder, nearly electrocuting what remained of him on the magnetic pull of the frayed cord.

The good people of Colorado Springs, where Tesla had lived, gathered in black on a rare day of rain and feared the light might one day even go out of their religion. The indigenous tribes of Cheyenne Mountain journeyed to Pikes Peak to try to capture afternoon lightning, though they knew the Peak by names less certain of posterity. Nocturnal animals shifted from *possums* to *opossums*, *stink badgers* to *skunks*, blaming rogue sparks of moonlight in the not-yet-buried sun for their confused callings. *Tesla had died as he had died*, the barn owl hooted all light long. *He will live, now, also as he has died.*

Nikolai and Pavlo and Yuri left the saloon and wondered why lamps in their mining hats had dimmed. Why their words were somehow stuck in their throats, even after shots of whiskey and a beer back. The poets spoke in the strange way poets speak: Karl Marx proclaimed, *Death is the opiate of the people*; Henry David Thoreau responded, *Eat the woods before the woods eat you*; Carl Sandburg guarded the grave and kept calling everyone *Hog Butcher* in the most adorable way; and Vallejo—Vallejo said nothing, fingering, instead, the outline of his skeleton through a suit coat that had grown too large, a skeleton he had washed every day, that somehow in Tesla's death glowed in Paris or Peru with the aurora borealis of a life well-deathed.

At Fort Morgan

Who can say when we die—
or if? Call me Fort Morgan.
I'm ready for dust and dirt.
The hungry bees of the soil
turn over centuries
of nomadic paths
in my blood. I have driven
here for the day just to feel the ache of the plains
only to taste the lonely blood notes of late summer.
Someone keeps trying to call to me
through my own bones. There is a vibration
of canary song, goldfinch chatter both here
and seventy-six miles southwest in Denver,
and over to Cimarron and Kimball.
They keep saying, swaying,
Don't stay here; always remember, the tree
drops its leaves in order for them to scatter.
And I know this is where I should stay
only as long as my tongue—blessèd root—allows.
Something keeps tugging, telling me my life
is wrong. That it is time to beckon forward
from the complicated bees
in my blood a brace of hounds to scour
the base of sycamores and oaks. Those Fort Wayne trees
bend cottonwoods here in Fort Morgan,
my voice ravined in a Colorado wind hollow
among starving farms, empty stores, and boarded doors.
Who can say if the trees are nailed shut and will survive
my life, or even the wind's death? Or if my breath

will sink into the emotional depths
of their roots? Where years of grief gather,
the sky here is somehow soothingly blue. This is the land
of smoke and lack of rain. Ancients ago
the river said, *Listen.* The South Platte flowed
at least three and one-third times my mouth.
How to measure the fate and forgiveness of water.
How I've wept my head more nights
than I can count, the wind scraping my name.
How the dappled rumps of Appaloosas
are actually starlight that came in secret
one night to visit and never left.

At the Abbey of St. Walburga, Virginia Dale, Colorado

August 1, 2023, Full Sturgeon Moon

The nuns are darning socks again
In the cruel moonlight
Once when I was a church mouse
I ate nothing but owl bones
I traveled through the bodies
Of those who would hate me
We eat everything beneath the full white moon
Including its damp willowy hair
We pass through Virginia Dale
The old Overland Stage Station
Population 1,073
Past Ranch Springs Road and Cherokee Park
On the road to Tie Siding
Stop at the Abbey
We quiet we comfort we calm
We become different we become who we thought
We were always meant to be
Just a stone's throw from my home
By chance
Is this house of prayer on the Colorado-Wyoming border
As if it is an extension of my body
As if it *is* my body
As if wolf blood coyote gait
Howling out into the ever-blistering wind
Whipping from Tie Siding down from Laramie
There are holes in my bones

Flute sounds I wish the Sisters could mend
Turning the sock of my life inside out
One thought from their contemplative glance
Could spiral out
Into Bosque elms
Aspen
The muddled pandemonium among the ruffled needles
Of flummoxed ponderosa pine
Could bring water up from an undug well
Could bring back the owls cracking mice bone
Beneath a cloud-banked moon
As if the darkness hidden in all things
Remains
The darkness hidden in all things
Traveling through the breastbone of an owl
Perched compass north
Here in Virginia Dale at the Abbey
And shivering through the thinly thick animal night
In the unforgiving wailing of the wind-drenched wind

The Long Death of Doc Holliday

1851–1887

He was not a real doctor but a man of teeth.
And because the townsfolk could barely breathe,
they paid little heed to teeth. The cough. It was the cough

that caught him. He began gambling, he said,
    when patients left his office, fearing the disease.
Dodge City was not a frontier town for long. It's highly

unlikely that Big Nose Kate was present at his death,
    though the thought of having a prostitute from
Hungary as a common-law wife entranced every one of them.

The sanatorium in those days was quiet. Except for the cough.
    The constant hack hack bloodletting from each
of their rooms. Consumption, they say, fares better in thin air.

And so Glenwood Springs, Colorado. And so the sad mules
    slowly up the hill. And so Wyatt Earp bringing him
there after the vendetta was settled. The Hotel Colorado,

an unlikely place to die. And Big Nose Kate present
    at this death, they say, though they never laid eyes.
He told them more than once of Tombstone, of the arid grace

of Arizona Territory, of the Gunfight at the O.K. Corral.
    Thirty shots in thirty seconds at 3:03 p.m. He was troubled
by numbers. Numb to symmetry. Doc with a double-barreled

shotgun under his longcoat. Forever after, he complained
        of a possum permanently lodged in his chest,
a porcupine positioned against his rib. Was it the disease

or the men he killed at close range? And when he could not
        clear his phlegm halfway through the telling, all
the townsfolk cleared their throat, a little, for him, swallowing

back a bit of his blame. Not a real doctor, they'd whisper
        later in the hall, but a man of death. Fixing teeth,
dealing faro, stepping out into the bullet-filled street

in an attempt to die. *Death can be quick or slow*, he'd say
        each morning, razor hard against the strop, as if he
could slit his own throat, as if lamenting surviving the fight.

What one keeps hidden in a longcoat looms large. Like life
        in the chest. A depth of breaths. The woman.
It was the woman who tended him. Dabbing blood-trickle

from his nose. Only a common-law wife from Hungary
        would have no fear. It's highly unlikely the fight
was fair. Virgil, Wyatt, and Morgan Earp were badass law.

It was the woman in Bauer's Butcher Shop two blocks
        from the corral who spoke against Doc and the Earps,
hanging the meat out to dry. The hack hack hacking

of the pig's limbs. It was the knife that caught it, deep
        belly-slit before the blood. It's highly unlikely
they'll survive—any of the townsfolk—the night. It comes

red down the throat as they breathe the seeming deep of sleep,
    trying to forget their shame. Like wine. Like broken
blood. Like water from the healing springs. Thirty swigs

in thirty minutes. The way any cleansing comes from the earth
    that otherwise absorbs everything. Keeps every human
pain. What we secretly keep in our longcoats. What we feast.

What fast we draw upon the law. The law of live or life.
    Of don't-say-die. Of a many-years'-hacking and how
it shaped a man's life. A gunslinger who died in bed with his

boots *off*, reportedly laughing at himself. His final phrase,
    Now that's funny, winging west over the peaks. Only age
thirty-six, and the November wet—the *forever* wet—of leaves.

501 Words West of Wichita

The first disappointment to the citizens of Dodge
    was to grant jurisdiction to their desires.
For prostitution. Whiskey. Faro. Incidents such as these
    made people believe the sensual presence of animal
ghosts. Coyotes, cougars, horses. Word crawled down
    from the Medicine Bows that the horse was alive,
there in Laramie, 655 miles away. And it was. In our words.
    In the mouth as we soaked them. In kerosene rags.
One consonant. One vowel. In the syllables of almost-love.
    In the teabag on the counter. The ginseng kitchen
painted green. *Moles is awful bad on 'sang*, Wallace Moore
    had said, from the hills of northern Georgia. *They'll eat
the root, a mole will.* So will our words. All 501 of them, pulling
    apart the dead belly of a crow. On the Rawhide Flats,
a bull or cow is easy to eye-gouge. Gender doesn't matter
    when we sink our speak. Into the intestine of another,
we call our words crawling back like specks of bread.

Little is known of the habits of the Wichita ant. How it travels
    miles unsuspectingly in a Pontiac or Ford.
In a grocery bag. Through time zones of change. Hidden
    along the ridge of a mirror in a woman's compact.
I have occasionally seen one returning to the nest as if it were
    necessary to remove midnight from day, hiding its
black-bodied self under a stick or root. The long night long,
    light goes on brightening the dread. Our language
languishing two horse lengths behind. Prostitutes proselytize.
    Faro dealers fold. Sunflowers bow to one another
as if no longer locked in a singular stalk of swaying talk.

Consequently, even Bat Masterson had to leave
Wichita decades before, under hover of night, on the loping
rails west, ginseng root at his tooth.

The second disappointment to the people of Dodge
    was in the saloons. In the streets. The lawless dark.
Sometimes this led to descriptions of certain women as *Ladies
    of the Blight*. To south-central Kansas as *God*. Other
times, as *a lightning fire fierce across the plains*. Word magic,
    Cassirer called it, from as far off as French
Equatorial Africa where the dance if danced just right
    made even the rain rain. What we say might be?
How we hurt might not? Words crawl down the snowy Bows
    as Big Medicine. Lodge in our throats. Ask us things
we swear we'd never repeat, even in crowds. Or do, except
    if we married wrong the right person. In Laramie.
In Wichita. In the 655 miles in between. Incidents
    such as these made my ghost horse stir, paw the dirt.
There, there, I'd tell it, patting it, as if its vapor were hide.
    As if I'd stirred it with a word. Diction dictating
jurisprudence? *Women are men and men are deer flies
    biting back the dark weather*, Wallace Moore
might think but never say. At least in private
    before the fire. Every house, even hovel, has a pile
of dried buffalo manure for fueling the mouth
    ·   in a Godless country.

The Last Jump

Since the filming of Jesse James, released in 1939, "No animals were harmed in the making of this motion picture."

There are no words   for how she felt. We each feel,
    feeling into,
        falling through. There is no great
abyss.   There are hounds and graves
and great   sighs   in Dakota.
In Williston. Right there   in Northfield, Minnesota,
and in the somehow-widening   Missouri Breaks.
So much death by accident of chance. How can the mouse
trembling in talons   slurch such wisdom
       this way, that?

The terrible rippings of the rain   are spokes of flesh,
sun falling through   the tiniest creatures of the cliff.
They took the ridge   and greased the chute.
    They sat the horse. The stuntman
clutched the cantle.   They felt the saddle horn
adorn. Marveled   at their virility,   at the power
of a truck engine,   how many mustangs'-worth
of drive it takes   to haul a camera to the top. Face it.
We all like power,   even if it's just the decision to survive.
Even if we're only allowed   *Tyrone* Power,
starring in a film, as Jesse James.   Outlaw strength
against the force of restraint.

    There are words.   There are no words.
The horse could not talk.   It felt, in the slippery tilt chute,

feeling far into itself   far as the eye could
bleed. And it *does* at high altitudes.   Tiny vessels of rain
bursting into sunspots   in the filming of the scene.
Offerings at the table of dark   and blight.
We're fond of such   opposites. That's why we need a man
named Fonda   to play Jesse's older brother, Frank.

Okay, *I'll* be frank. It hurt. Hurts.   Just to watch. To see
the horse so utterly stumped,   tumbling over
the edge,   turning once,   twice,
                                   dropping
its scared and trembling self   seventy feet
into the lake. Its feet   flailing   wildly
as if to show   no hope   for the humble. Even
Nancy Kelly,   as Jesse's lover, Zerelda Cobb,
      could not save the scene. Eyebrows plucked, arched,
as if eighteen   and beautiful in 1939   somehow made
jumping off a ledge   desirable. We jump for many
a suggestive smile,   silky blonde hair seizing mostly moon
as if pawing   the rich   mineral rinse   in the almost-
dark. There is also the matter   of staying alive. Even if we
survive the fall.   Into ourselves. Into one another.   Into
the world.   As did the horse, landing squarely in the lake.

But the panic-thrash,   uncontrolled, as she drowned
before the hostlers   could reach a rope. Years before,
she would stunt. Saunter   —not trot—   they say,
toward the back of an arena.   In Livingston, Montana.
In Reno. In the scrabble
                  down a hill.   Side to side,
she would sway,   in perfect horse step. One shoe, two.
Then the echo   of all those centuries   of canyon.

A flak of falling rock.　　　In Denver.　　North Platte.
In Ogallala. All those years　　　she had known exactly
what to do.　　　Impulse-twitch, as if fly-swatting
with her tail　　　through the raccoon rings　　of sleep.
Even through the rough　　　of Randolph Scott,
who played Marshall Will Right,　　tracking Tyrone Power.
Power　　　powering itself　　　　to the top.
To a dead end.　　To a horse fettered by fright.
Not fifty yards　　　in front of Marshall Will Right.
What is *right*,　we rarely know.　　What we *will*,
is left at the edge,　　with our stunt double surviving the fall.
Mouse-wail snap　　　in the talon of an owl.
The terrible ripping　　　　of the rain.
　　　　The terrible gripping of the reins.

Abandoned Cabin

*San Luis, oldest town in Colorado,
on the border of New Mexico*

I felt the death axe in my hand. My blood,
for one thing, was alive still as the chain
from the bear trap rusting the wall. The bones
of a woman cried out somewhere east,
an unread book on the bed. Something unopened
made the kitchen hungry, as if the dead
wanted food only I could provide.

To whom did this cabin belong?
I won't say it was dark. Light
from the setting sun suggests the coming
of blood, of moon, a lake somewhere north,
with dead mules that had never learned to swim.
Surely, the man who homesteaded here
had been lonely, old as the oldest town
in Colorado. How do the dead measure love
if not in bear traps and rust, teeth gnarling
from the wall? What memory of slow
purposeful steps resides in rawhide lacings
of snowshoes that have stepped away from winter,
marking the yard one hundred years back?

Let the whole valley die of autumn,
if you ask me. These slack months
have caught me somewhere between hardtack
and headache. Take a bite of your own death

nailed to a wall. I won't complain. Fall is dead
because we've lost the grace to call it autumn,
lying stiff in the bottom of some creek
conjugating grief with gold leaves. I won't celebrate
the roof's collapse or the ritual burning
of trees. Can't imagine how piercingly
the horses must have whinnied, the mules
going mosquito-mad.

                      For two hours a hawk
has circled, and some large black bird keeps stiffening
my voice. Three snow geese north, my life
forms the border of a town that until 1861
was in the Territory of New Mexico.
In San Luis, I am always two places
at once and always saying goodbye. Goodbye,
Indiana. Goodbye, Colorado. Goodbye
to this place of grief I hold as cold stones
and muzzling bones. Abandoned
might mean full. Something was left here
when everything was taken. I want to move.
I want to stay here forever.
This is how you say hello to your past.
Goodbye. Adios. Goodbye.

The Mining Camps of the Mouth

He spoke with words that had been held before
    in the mouths of the dead. Words like *wistful*
and *wildfire*. In the mining camps of the Medicine Bows,
    every healing hurts. *Once, when I was young, I was dead,*
said the man about to be my life. The mouth moistens
    hard as hands gone sad. At least in Hygiene
in high-country summer. Where the consumptive come
    to coax the air. All going comes to Colorado.
All coming leaves desire decried. There is no paradox
    up high when one stinks of the inner depths.
Despair is overrated, I heard slantwise through the throat
    of the many-soaked. *Why it rhymes with "repair"*
is one of the Seven Wonders of the World. One of my many pasts
    had finally caught up with me. Reed-bound,
mummified. It spoke, she spoke, he smoked in a barrel
    of water his last severe brand. Against the leaning shed,
where calves moaned *no*, they stacked the hot iron, sizzling
    with names. Not names but pictographs. Not graphs
but hieroglyphs from deep within the ranch: *The Oxbow;*
    The Circle Shade; The West-of-Dodge. Honestly, I read
one word at a time, one line of burnt hide. Note: instructions
    for how to be alive: draw each brand, with precision,
before your cowboy license is revoked. Note: instructions
    for how to be dead: *be* dead.

What burns into us our saddle-tramp name is new leather
    creaking old. Ore bags slung over the rump of a mule.
Poor things are sterile, you know. Like any offspring

of a donkey and a willow. Get yourself a horse.
Lead it to water. Make it stink. *You* try sitting unshaven
            for eighty-nine days on the cattle drive from Abilene
to Dodge and see if your inner creaking is leather or gold.
        I spoke with words that had been held before in
mysterious folds. Words like *love* and *touch*. Words like *bled*
        and *dead*. In the mining camps of my mouth, I kept
bending over a pan of the purest gold. Leaping up into me
        like wildfire. Even at high altitude columbine grow.
The lung is an amazing organ. An origami crane in the chest.
        We need new names just to breathe. Names
of destruction and love. Names that wing us into the ever-
            hopeful West. Names that send our unexamined stool
samples to Hygiene. To correct our tubercular tense—past,
            present, and nerves. Names that are ranch-hand sad.

There are, of course, Seven Wonders of both the Ancient
            and Modern Worlds. There's the Temple of Artemis
at Ephesus, of course. Chronicled by Callimachus of Cyrene.
        Which sounds remarkably like *Kalamaras of Serene*.
The serenity, of course, of burying a burro on the high country
            pass. Something tender and dear and sad is always
carrying us up and over ourselves, into the time of no crime
            and many soothing sheep. Not names, but hands.
Not hands, but a new kind of ranch: *The I've-Been-a-Jerk;
        The Oh-I'm-Sorry; The Will-I-Ever-Find?* Honestly, I bled
one syllable, one word at a time. Note: instructions for how
        to love: it spoke, she spoke, *he* spoke. Note:
instructions for how to be alive: *Be* alive; coax the folds
        of your tongue, the words that had been before
in the everlasting mouths of the dead.

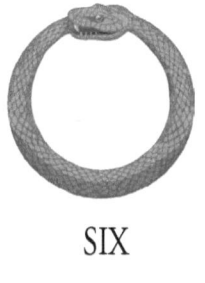

SIX
THE SOMNAMBULIST DREAMS

Dream in Which John Haines and I Homestead Together in Alaska

1.
Somehow, we're working together in 1947—his first year at the Richardson homestead at Milepost 68, outside Fairbanks. We've spent the day minding our trapline, and Haines seems peeved I released some animals. Kissed them, then just let them go. He warns me about the cold and how we'll need those pelts not just for trade but to make hats and mittens against the coming snows.

Then we're back at our cabin, eating moose stew, and I tell him about the moose release site in Colorado, just up the road from my house. He doesn't seem to hear. Maybe he doesn't care? He seems to be listening to music, tapping his foot, tilting his head this way, that, though the only thing I can hear is wind whingeing through the slats of our log cabin.

He blows out the kerosene lamp on the table next to an open book of poems by Du Fu. Stokes the fire once more, then grabs the top bunk, leaving me the bottom. I pull the animal hide tight against my chin, listening to the wind. Shivering. Yes, it's me shivering, not the wind. Though it could just as well be our cabin. And in its moaning it almost sounds human. Desperately human. Then I hear Haines reciting the poems of Du Fu, as if reading from the book on the table across the room. But he's memorized them and recites them from his bunk as if singing a lullaby, trying to calm me. Somehow, his years of wandering soothe. Du Fu's wandering soothes. Somehow, the endless wars and Du Fu's exiles to China's remote north soothe. Even the death of the little oriole that used to perch on his windowsill spring mornings.

2.
Then the world is spinning, heavily. I begin to sink into the waters of sleep, listening to Haines recite then chant Du Fu. I can sense that tomorrow might not *be* tomorrow but could be yesterday or even the day before. That mushing huskies with Haines might take me back years. Decades even. To an afternoon with Sergeant Preston of the Yukon and his lead dog, Yukon King. Was there really a land bridge from Alaska to Siberia and China? How many times—and in which life— did I walk across? And in which direction? What animals did I love, and why?

Now he is snoring. John Haines is snoring, though even his sleep breath is melodious. *I could ride that sound forever*, I think. *Take Du Fu with me wherever I go. Walk with his words even across the sea into the cold breaches of Siberia where Gogol is waiting to lend me his overcoat. Where Dostoevsky whispers my name as he keeps plowing the dark with handkerchief and knife.*

Somehow, it's morning, and the stars keep bearing upon me, shifting positions. Their alignments say things I can't quite discern. Haines and I take a good long piss together beneath the new dawn moon. Steam rising from the snow at our feet. The dogs are frantic, urgently barking and clanging their chains, longing for a day of lugging along the banks of the Yukon. I rub sleep from my eyes. The world blurred. And Haines is already ahead of me, harnessing the dogs, reciting to them a Du Fu poem about a cat who claimed a tree. About a donkey who carried his daughter and him over a hill in Yunnan, nearly to the capital.

The Yukon River seems close. I see its tributaries in the veins of my unclad arm—even though I'm fully clothed in caribou skins and mukluks. I keep thinking I could scour those trails. Follow those traplines like star charts down my arm. Mush the measure of my own blood. From there on the Yukon. Down into Colorado. Through the Snowies. Through the Mummies. And into the Rawahs. All the way home.

SEVEN

NOCTURNE
OF THE WESTERN NIGHT

Now That the Owls Have Gone

After the wildfire, the owls have gone.
For years, in the pines outside my study,
I'd hear the moon pouring through their voice.
The world could have ended across the river
a thousand times my mouth. The sky
could have shifted. Rocks could have
given into a snowy drift.

Now the pines are gone, and with them
the wildest of our work. Days echo
in the barren grass, though the deer are back
and the bobcats and the bears. But the owls,
whom I love, have stayed away for lack of trees,
though the grass be rich with snakes and mice.

I have weighed the heaviness of the foxes
behind our house scurrying to den their young before
the storms. I have witnessed the afternoon rains.
The calming of fog. The way a cloud
contains fire signs north from Laramie and Cheyenne.
I have measured my words to the breathing
of birds, prayed for the hooting
and pine perching to return.
For the treeless ground outside our rebuilt home
to meet the empty place inside me with a sudden wing-beat
of peril and purpose, and a forest sound
so drenched in midnight that day has no choice
but to break. Open. Drying in the early slant
of sun. Over and again.

I Heard a Primitive Sadness
from My Primordial Mouth

This is the season of death and dry air.
On this rise, I call the owl
dark across my mouth.
I dreamed the rocks were alive.
And when I awoke, they were.
Now, the fire ants in mounds around them
build tiny pyramids pointing north
to ease the passage through.
Scattered in these Colorado mountains are the bones
and ash of mountain lions, coyotes, and bears.
The wild turkeys here on Turkey Roost Drive
are gone, having figured it was best
not to be the national bird after all,
kiting away from Franklin and the founders
and everything their feathers could have been.
They are dreaming of bawl-mouthed hounds in Indiana
hollers or lolling outside dilapidated porches
and tobacco barns in Kentucky that keep wheezing
through busted boards and weathered ribs.
How long can our bodies hang on
to the desire to hold the moon in our throat?
How many times can we dung-roll our words
phrase to phrase, hoping for the best?
Mouthing the word *now* to finally get things right?

This is the season of dead water. Of dry air
looting the lung. Of cursing the lack of snowmelt
from the Medicine Bows and Mummy Range.

I come to this place to hear myself bleed,
one owl feather, one tuft of fox fur, at a time.
To tell myself the sky is right
to go on forever, north from our home
in Livermore, into Wyoming
past Rawlins and the Bighorns. And further,
into Montana, through Whitefish and Glacier.
And on into Medicine Hat. In Canada.
To work my words whole, hold each vowel
as seed sounds in my mouth.
To dream of rocks waking themselves
true north into moon both and now.
To hold onto clouds calibrating the sky,
those clouds that accept dry weather as dry
and hold onto the rain that doesn't ever
quite reach the ground.

Rain All Night in the Rain

The rain is raining again.
It always seems to rain *rain*.
Somehow, parts of ourselves
flake off, but they don't look like me.
They resemble barnacles
that have been traveling a long way.
I have kept them hidden
in sea stain and mold. Yes,
I adore the color green. Even this
muck that has clung there so long
beneath me. I had thought
it had helped me stay afloat,
until I realized its layers and weight.
Color isn't always heavy.
When the moon is golden,
freshly full, the world is right.
When the sugar maples bleed,
I am inside them. Full
and flourishing. I sap my strength
with too much worry. I stay up late
listening to the rain,
wondering what is inside it
since books tell me there is always something
inside something else. Am I living
in the West or in a place *inside*
the West? Are these ponderosa and lodge pole
pines actually pine trees or branches
inside cottonwoods coaxing the river?
What does Colorado hold

deep in its folds? The rain keeps raining
rain, all night in the rain. I ask forgiveness
for what is wet and more wet. For the furry growths
that are uncontrollably green at the bottom
of my seeing. For what is inside
the insides of me.

The Agony of the Leaves

If it isn't the sky widening
its lightning mouth. If it isn't
turkey vultures circling, calling
our names from inside my chest.
Then it's air crowding the air.
Then it's the sun about to crush itself
into the powdered glass of dusk.
Then it's everything I had thought
possible somehow clawing its way back
into me through the breastbone of a hawk.

We were both strangers to one another, you and I.
All three of us contained daytime bits
of broken moons. You, me, and the hawk.
All four, even five, of us (if we count the night
grass and the moon lodged therein) knew better
than to ever leave the West. Or to even try.

Come count with me the white hairs on the wrist
of the old poet I loved. Call her, *Woman
Who Taught Me to Never Fear a Falling Tree.*
Call him, *Here, Hold This Wristwatch and Go
to the River to Measure the Absolute Depth
of Despair.* Call them together,
*The Wolves Inside My Chest Writing a Poem
with Each Breath Released.* Come
console the badgers on the Laramie Plains
near Cheyenne to remain
tucked yet vigilant in their dens,

the sow close to the hole guarding
her cubs from midnight
seeping through. Come ask of me my mouth
if it might finally be okay for each
of my words to splinter and shift.

If it's not the rain, then it's the rain
stuck in a cloud. If it's not the wind
housed in my mouth, then it's the moon sobering
the dark. If it's not these words, these sounds,
then it's the pouring of boiling water,
the agony of the leaves as I try to rinse the world
of pain. As I rise in the morning to look up
into the underbellies of birds—splotches of starlight
still there in the speckles of their daytime flight—
and do something as simple as measure a tablespoon
of leaves into a bowl. Breathe upon them
the anticipation of the day. Pray over the water
with gratitude for the pain the leaves
are about to receive. And steep a pot of tea.

When Lightning Bugs Become the Stars

Tonight, the moon is crossing
the Yampa River, and the sky
and world are right. Stars plunge
themselves into the riverbank
and scrabble of gravel. There is always
more than one way to slurp the sap
of stars. Back then, as a child,
I would go out to catch fireflies
in the Indiana dusk, and when stars
appeared, I was certain the lightning
bugs had gone off, leaving *me* to light
the world. Now, when I hold the moon
in my throat, I know the cold snows
of the north and the long months
to get there. I know when the coyote
howls here in Livermore that there is
a pack of wolves in Manitoba
trying to reach me. I know the fox
denning behind our house
has traveled from Japan, from inside
a book in which she was also a courtesan
magically transformed by a kiss.
That my bed sheets and their snug flannel
contain a weather vane pouring the wind
from the north, from a boreal forest
in which I am lost both and found.
The weathercock turns and turns
in ways that show me how easy it is
to lose direction. How I need to keep

looking down into the fertile ground—
where the glowworm descends into the dirt—
to know where my light is
and how to reach it.
And to learn, from below, just how to fly.

Early Autumn Darkness, Livermore, Colorado

The days are getting shorter like a life beginning to thin
Years before, I asked my mother, *Which way to the calendar of shade?*
When she spoke, she spoke slow, not slowly
The world has always been beginning to end
That's the way it is with sunlight
It is often overanxious to burn itself out
If I don't go to bed on time
If I don't go to bed now
The wind might stop
And then the earth might shake
Down in the water wells small living things begin to breathe
The ants keep trying to climb the steep bricks
And burst out of themselves
Mayflies borrow the sun a month or more a year
Moths may capture the moon's furry eye in their wing
The night is long, so long the darkness begins
To slow, even the night growing tired of itself
The darkness begins to slow
Telling itself about itself
All light long

Some Mornings

1.
Some mornings the world feels right. You wake as if you'd been dead. A long time or short, it doesn't matter. It just feels good to rise, to dislodge the swirling tumbleweed from the back of the throat. Even the gutters of the house seem clean. The bird droppings on the south-facing window are oddly comforting. From which bird did they come? A crow? A golden eagle? Black or gold, it is still the same. The sun comes up or it doesn't, but it doesn't matter. You have endured the engulfment of the night and the hawk talons tearing at your chest.

2.
Other mornings appear as if to say, *I'm sorry. We don't mean to disturb, but time for you to come on in from the dark of sleep and face even more dark.* It may be raining or not. A good book is waiting on the kitchen table, half-open, unable to finish reading itself, and you are powerless to help, incapable of even remembering where you were in the Icelandic mystery you'd been reading and how to move forward. Or how dark it was at the close of the previous chapter when within twenty-four hours the sun barely rose. Or how much snow clogged the moor. But you're certain someone shot someone or something. Took something away. Either in the book or from you and what you can barely detect from peering into the dead mountain air where you live, where only turkey vultures circle.

Your fear perplexes. Self-indicts. Makes you want to bang your head against anything solid. Even your own head, if that were possible. Colorado, you know, is beautiful. Just look out the window. You could be beautiful too, if you could just dump this mood. And you're longing again for bed. And the darkness. Or a really good kiss. Or any touch at all. Anything to stoke the senses. Placate your mood. Maybe a cinnamon roll. French toast. Even chocolate or honey.

3.
Finally, the day dissolves. The hours dissolve. The moon appears. Rain begins or ends. Your wife starts dinner. Some lovely scent of saffron and coriander fills the house from the cookstove. Some mornings are not quite mornings. This is autumn. This is evening. This is what it means to feel alive. The fox kits in back of the house cry out, and you understand their hunger not so much as longing but as that part of you you'd earlier wept off. The eternal cycle of black and gold feels close. Purposeful. Even in the fluffy young of their coats. The world outside, silent and comforting. Birch smoke seeping in from neighbors heating their evening.

You scan the drizzly rinse of rain and gray. Realize that (except for your hair) you're not gray at all. And never have been. Perhaps there is a red-tailed hawk. Perhaps an owl, whose wing-whoosh makes your favorite sound. There's a bite to the air. An almost-hint of snow. And the good of the world is good again. The moon's sorrow nearly topples you with joy. Its ruinous white waves bathe you and soothe when you consider Du Fu sailing up the Milo centuries before, accepting his aching legs and white hair. You are grateful he came to teach you to see and hear and be more fully human. Iceland seems further away and colder. The Colorado darkness surrounds, outline of mountains sinking into the earth. You take the moon's lozenge under your tongue, easing it down your throat. Forget the mystery you'd been reading, still open on the table beside you, and peer into the deepening dark of evening darkness, singing into the still, black sky. Not needing to solve a single thing.

This Hour

1.
Up all night again. Blaisie asleep
at my side by the fire. Autumn
whirls in once more here in the mountains.
So much of me is gone, even as I find more
of myself in these late middle years.
The turkey vultures earlier today circled
over and again above our little home
on Turkey Roost Drive. What dead are they
after? What dead did they find in finding themselves?
What is dead inside these walls—of my house, say,
and of my body? Time eats itself away at 3:08 a.m.,
bitten by starlight, salved by the yowling of a bobcat.
Soon it will be 4:17 and 2:28 at once.

                                        Life is like that—
forward and back. Indiana is dead and dying as the fox kits
behind the house whimper and whine for their mother
to bring more food. Blaisie hears them, cocks her beagle head.
The wind halts a moment then resumes its wailing.
Surely, the prairie grass an hour away in Laramie
is crying out to be wind-combed over and again,
for me to walk barefoot back the years,
for me to understand the caution of blisters,
the necessity of slowing my stride.
I have been there, and I am back, absorbed now
in autumn wind. Its death grip and release.
A thousand summers have come and gone,
and at least a thousand more before that

since Alexander the Great climbed down
from his horse, sat the dust, and spoke
privately with a naked sadhu in India
who somehow convinced him to turn back.
And as he turned his armies
he somehow moved forward for home?
The wind rises and falls, mimicking the whining
of the fox kits for food, the stirring of dirt inside me.

2.
How could Kropotkin, after writing *The Conquest*
    of Bread, have endured so many years
of starvation? The wind disturbs yet quiets the night,
    calming my heart even as it tightens
with the creaking of the house. Surely, Alexander clarified
    his breathing as he focused on it moving
in and out prior to dying on the plains of pneumonia.
    As if the *Plains of Pneumonia* were a place.
An archeology of death. The Iranian plateau was unforgiving,
    even to the sun. Which blazed upon it and blistered.
Kropotkin, too, coughing up blood on his cot in Dmitrov,
    struggling to breathe, after he tried to explain to Lenin
why he supported Western entry into the First World War,
    siding—as he had—with England and France.

3.
Now, the turkey vultures circle
and will return tomorrow. *All this*,
Rexroth said, *will never be again*. And I am
with him tonight—even though he has left the body—

as I reread the way he breathed. The pauses.
The pressure. Light combing his Sierras. The Snowy
Mountain Range here, outside my window. My head heavy
like Rexroth's *brain . . . worried and tired*, until he reread
the entire set of encyclopedias—as he did each year—
the volume GIC to HAR reminding him
of seeing his first grosbeak
at Ten Mile Creek *Suffused with light*.

The autumn leaves keep falling. So much
of me is gone, dropping through
the still resinous earth, even as I find more of myself
in these late middle years in the whining
of foxes. In the disturbing distance of the stars.
They keep crawling at me with the heat
of a thousand and a thousand years that are both
here and gone tonight—this *entire* night—
as I sit with my beagle-hound before the burning
wood of the fire and the burning away of years.

When I Wept the Animal

*The wind is 95. It still pours from the east
like armies and it drains each day of hope.*
—Richard Hugo

The trains are gone. Deep in the mountain
night, I can only hear a bobcat's
yowl. Coyotes rustling the cheatgrass.
Down the draw, something is surely calling
my name. The wind is ninety-five tonight,
and at sixty-nine I am not too far behind.
I have been told that I need to be
told in ways which tell
the telling whole. Something is trying
to carry me away. And it's not the owls
who left after the fire, the Indiana trains far back
in my sleep. There were woods there and swamps
and the scent of wet dog and screeching
in the autumn leaves.

When I weep, I weep. When I wept
the animal, the animal wept me.

The Compassionate Darkness

with a first line by Rachel Peden

The compassionate darkness came in
It lodged in the throat
Like a hummingbird fluttering anthracite rain
We'd spent the day just trying to survive
This regret and that
The mountains kept trying to name us
Reflecting our various moods
Changing shape with the light
We knew something had to die
We knew even the light leaves us
A little empty
On those days when the sky darkens down
That we couldn't keep on like we had
I've spent my time searching among coyotes
In their wanderings
Their dens
Among their pungent scat
In the lonely places of their howling
Crying out to the moon pooling in puddles of late rain
For the midnight light to peel back and heal
The darkness was there since the first stirrings of my mouth
And deep inside that was a brood of bloodletting
Breaking benevolently like river rise carving stones
Over and across in rivulets among loose piles of gravel
In the shaded shallows
If I could release the give and grit
If I could release the grit of the world

I could absorb drops of light lodged there
Tender parts of myself flaking off
Among the autumn sandbars
That say the rain and snowmelt were not enough
That what we do is sometimes never enough
Though the compassionate darkness be there
Though the darkness like a lost sound
Like a regrettable echo
Hums and hovers
Coaxing us inward back and forth
Over and across with its midnight
Prairie pacing
Its moon-drenched dirt
With its sorrow-bound wing-snap
Dying back a little
The grueling fields that surround us
And threaten to consume

Nocturne of the Western Night

We thought the years would last forever,
They are all gone now, the days
We thought would not come for us are here.
—Kenneth Rexroth

Now that the night has bitten us
we understand the words
of those who came before. The creak.
We hear the creak of each syllable
among a stand of cedar. Juniper.
Fir. We come flying back through
each hole of our breathing. Core.
We know the moon. How could it have ever left us?
All those years it seemed to follow
when we drove town to town, embracing
its shadow. Council Bluffs. Ogallala.
North Platte. McCook. Sterling. Now,
it gives us only slushy snow. Cold. Uncaringly.
As if the radio could not find a voice.
As if the static of our lives. Stuck.
We understand the bodies of the almost-dead,
the bent and congestive, dragged up
from the swamp. Night shifts. Books
of food stamps. The twenty-four-hour market shelves
and fluorescent lights harnessing workers
to stock. Truckloads carrying the hours
away from everything we love. The world drove us
to this. The world and only the world
made it so. This is the way of slush and rain, a path

of dark clouds and sky. Laramie. Sheridan.
Casper. The long road up through the winding dark
of the Bighorns. The night keeps on
bearing the night. Starlight is buckshot
sprayed from the mouth of a god,
sometimes angry, sometimes asleep,
as she says, *I am with you always,*
and I am gone, broke and blistered
in the belly of the dark, in a cradle
of stars rocking through
the Milky Way. Nothing will remain
of the night except the night
clinging to the underside of our day
clothes, the way we speak, walk,
almost touch. Each word
burdened with what it holds onto
from the dark, barnacled and bent. Imagine
starlight camped in the mouth like rocks.
Imagine an all-night radio talk show saying nothing
but hurt. Imagine the only friend you have
in the long haul from Billings to Butte, Butte
to Missoula, Missoula to broke. The years we thought
would not come for us have come.
This is the dark. This is the night.
No wonder we keep trying to put it to sleep.

Lone Owl

Three a.m. Some stars. Night
sounds in the dark. Wind
hollowing out the cheatgrass.
The lamentations
of crickets. A few coyotes
yelping up to us from down
in the draw. Still, more
wind. And more.

Yet—I also hear the unexpected
purring of an owl. She is not outside
my window like thirteen years
ago but has returned
finally after the wildfire—
perhaps for this night only—
to the few remaining pines
down on Horse Mountain.

Her muted hooting
weaves through the wind,
seeming to calm it. And me.
How lonely three a.m.
has been for years
without her. How gorgeously
dark the darkness is
tonight inside me.

EIGHT
THE SOMNAMBULIST DREAMS

Dream in Which Frank Waters Is My Mother

It wasn't the bolo tie,
    though it did connect
        its umbilical cord self

to that mountain core
    of turquoise at his throat.
        Nor was it the way he made the morning

muffins, greeting me
    when I woke and descended
        the stair as if the word *oatmeal*

might save the world. *Burnt toast*,
    I'd told him, rubbing my eye. *In bed,*
        near my toes. And he sent me back

up to care for the crusts.
    When I returned, Frank
        was sewing a patch on my jeans.

As your mother, I must teach you. This is how
    my own mother did it when I was born many
        moons ago in Colorado Springs, he told me.

Here, hold this slip of thread
    between your lips, and try to keep it
        in place while mouthing the word "camel."

Dark parts of my scar
    were apparently flaking off.
        Frank acted as if I wasn't

becoming a man, as if the ripples
    in the sheets he'd change weekly
        were nothing but the water of stars

when they came to die.
    I sat and tried to smoke a rose,
        Frank telling me the thorns

would stunt my growth.
    That I should be careful
        to clean up any curve of burnt crust

my starlit body might cut.
    It's natural, he said. *Nothing*
        for shame. Remember, he continued,

it's easier for an antelope
    to pass through the eye of a crow
        than for a living man to be dead.

Somehow, he made sense. Frank Waters
    sense. As if my mother and divorced father
        were tiny rivulets I no longer needed

to ignore. From my core,
    a turquoise bolo suddenly around
        my *own* neck. Calming my throat.

The stone, he said, *Cerrillos turquoise.*
    It's such a shame. Now, the Cerrillos is
        completely mined out. Like the gold and silver

near Pikes Peak where I was born
    to my own pair of dark stars.
        I smelled oranges and saw Frank

pasting the glaze over a muffin.
    He'd put down the needle and thread
        and was carefully making a swirl.

This way, that. As if both
    ends of its sugary comet tail
        might collide at muffin's edge,

like a snake circling
    back to eat itself whole.
        This is the way of the Hopi,

he continued. *The ones who dance*
    the snakes and never get bit.
        Remember, it's easier to grieve

than to mouth the sound of now.
    He handed me his latest,
        his *Book of the Hopi,*

pointing to a passage on page 113.
    Then he sent me back up
        to care for the burnt crusts. *Careful,*

he said, *and be tender*
    with yourself. My body
        giving off dark drops

of watery stars
    like globs of gluey cold
        oats as I took the stair.

NINE

LOSING MYSELF IN THE LARGER MEASURE OF NOW

Once, When We Were Alive

We lived there once, among smooth brome and crested
wheatgrass. Right there on the banks of the North Fork
of the South Platte, where I was born
from the coupling of a cottonwood
and a river. The sound of the wind
was the wind, and we had floated with it westward
from Indiana. Something collapsed inside,
like a raccoon's bones as it squeezes through
the iron bars of a rain grate. The moon kept on
rising, on time of course, night after night,
over and again—sometimes larger, sometimes quiet,
calmed among crowded clouds. And all my former selves
died each time it shone golden, hidden
as if the first flower. To feel the lift and shift
in the beginnings of things was something the mountains
tried to teach. Was that the rise and fall
of an inland sea somehow buried centuries
on the high plains beneath buffalo grass? The stars
charted our future, revealing archaic threads, and our tongues
taught an inner astrology that documented the days
of the week as if they were historical events. Called out
to each star like old friends, forgotten. Prayed, that is,
to each day that we could somehow get to the next.
We had been told tales of old. True and untrue
stories of the Old West. We were to gnaw on each account,
we were instructed, for our own good. Even if just a yarn.
And we ate pieces of wind, shredded—it seemed—
just for us.

    When you slurp Monday's soup on Tuesday,

in what way does Wednesday open its flower heart
to you, turning its petals inside you like the pages
of a good book, a necessary book our gnawing needs
to know? Why does Thursday close down
around a thunderhead's dark gray anvil
forged on the horizon? How might Friday thirst
once and for maybe for the deep sleep
of Saturday and Sunday and become the rain
we have been long expecting? Even if it hovers there,
swampy dark in a cloud, and is just the rain
that doesn't reach—that never reaches—the ground?

New Moon, October

Coyotes over the ridge toward the Poudre tonight
are stirring the air with hunt and death.

You can hear the bleating of wind
through the cheatgrass. The tiny movements
of mice. Even their bones
bending the night. You can hear
the sound of the forest diminishing.

In the case of wilderness,
there is always the sound of a leaf
falling, the slippage of another blossoming.

Now the moon is trembling
like a person's last breaths on a slouching cot.
All they can hear is the clock murmuring
like animals that have been hiding,
moving in, now, through the underbrush.

Thinking of Bai Juyi on Yet
Another Day of Wind in Colorado

So many books on my shelves—
I choose one at random.
It could be Vallejo or Desnos
or even T'ao Ch'ien. The wind
keeps begging me
my sorrow. Down, perhaps,
from Cheyenne or Chugwater,
Sheridan or Cody. I open an anthology
to page 33 and see it is you.
These many years I've known you
as Po Chü-I, and now you are Bai Juyi,
the redemption of the romanization of *Hanyu
Pinyin* from the English-angled Wade-Giles.
So many years I beg you forgive me
my mouth. Forgive me in word
and deed. *Please*, I tell you, *stay well.
Don't have that stroke. Don't dress
in rags. I want your daughter to live.*
My middle name is William. Perhaps
I should take it as my surname, hover
near the end of the alphabet
with Burton Watson and Arthur Waley,
and translate your grief the way they did.
Perhaps I should reshape your words
so the world's sorrows no longer
need pass through your mouth.
The turkey vultures are once again circling
my home. Maybe they want me,

or more precisely my name. This shaking
of my roof and walls is a current
from Wyoming's Wind River Mountains
that carries even the dust
from the Sinks in the cavern floor.
And you are in it. Alive, again,
as *Po Chü-I* or *Bai Juyi*
or *Please-Forgive-Me-My-Mouth*.
And your daughter is there too—tender
little Golden Bells—allowed, finally,
to age. As is your wailing
infant son the typhus took.
And you are no longer
bent by the wind but are part of it
whipping through the grass
here in Livermore and back in Luoyang,
in the monastery at Longmen,
and here again in the keen eye
of the vulture that has left
its circle of feathers
to follow wind drafts down the draw.
Your beautiful words floating on and on
all these centuries late without sorrow
or age or a life given you
as air pockets—a test
of turbulent syllables—
so you could learn to mend the wailing
of the world. The holes
in your robe.

Back There in the Old Days

*Back there in the old days I was
a tree, a cottonwood on an empty lot.*
—William Stafford

Back there in the old days, the world was new.
And I was new, not yet quite knowing
how old old really was. Back there,
the sky bled broken plates of moon.
And when the wind rose, something in us fell
as if seeking balance. Back in the old days,
I dreamed of living in the West. And I carried
a photo of a buffalo jump pinned to my vest
with a note saying, *Let's all fall together over
the rocky edge and savor the delicate organs
of the steaming meat.*

Back in the old days, there was there,
and here was here. Sometimes there was here,
and here was nowhere to be found.

Back there—way back—I was a tree, a shagbark hickory
peeling away from my true core. Parts of me
were coming unstuck, and the whole world
was partially torn as a means to heal.
Back there in the old days, I could remember my name,
and it went something like this: *A cottonwood
and a river made a child from the most tender way
they coupled on a moonlit bank.* When the world ached,
I ached. And I knew I was alive
by the depth of my hurt.

Back in the old days, I was very old,
even when the world was young.
Even when *I* was young.
The world and I were so young that we forgot
we were old. And the trees of the world
were people and animals who did not believe
in charms. Back, before magic
was called that, what we said
was made manifest, even when spoken
in passive voice. And the cottonwood that became
my life was as ebullient as goldfish swimming
in the canary grass. The leaves captured the sun
and cured the moon in a small shack
over burning beech logs. And the ache
of the world—the whole of it—
went something like this: *I was born
in the tender moon-leaves of a river,
which rose in me and fell. Which keeps
rising and falling beneath the blessèd
blistering of the moon
camped in the waves—
always new, always bruised.*

Ghost Town Train Stop on the "Old Prairie Dog Express" of the Burlington & Missouri River Railroad

Here, in northeastern Colorado, you leave
the dead for dead. Nothing good at your feet
but dirt. Two buttes swell from out of the plains
like a dichotomous lie. Your entire life
you've struggled to survive sun strain and rock.
In the Pawnee Grasslands you wonder
where is the railroad, and where is the ghost town
of Keota? Where are its saloon-shuttered
spirits, and why must we die?
Towns this far north nudge the Wyoming
border and are wind-banging bad. The sun,
here, seems to come up in the north
along with a fleck of rock-breathing rain
where the fossilized three-toed horse
was preceded by ancient camels who could live
without water for weeks. On this day
of blistering sun, they show you how not
to hold the throat. So, you've said too much
for far too many? So, eagles, hawks,
and falcons fierce their nests on the butte
ledges as if a brushfire in your hair?
Wind in your belly asks why just two buttes,
says dichotomy today might be right, urges
live or *left*, *rise* or *die*. Antelope flee
the heat-pounding ground of now. Dung beetles
somehow roll your name, clasped in an insistent
fly-twitch of tail.

Before the railroad,
the Pawnee kept many horses
and daughters. They were beautiful,
painted for war, and drove the sons mad.
Who is this "they" when we are fumbling
fiercely for words? Perhaps *you* is *I*, and *they*
are *me*? So much gets confusing fast. Especially
when new tenses take hold and contract.
Words invert in the numb act of naming.
Columns of sandstone stand 300-feet high.
They could leave your body here, you think, filthy
and fierce among the birds. As if you were
a Parsi in Mumbai, coaxing the vultures
home. First an eyeball, then a finger, then a groin.

You have come here to the site of the "Old Prairie
Dog Express" to leave the dead for dead.
There *is* no *express* when we live our lives
in the long way down. There, in the distance,
you watch a beak tear the tongue
of a rabbit, unlucky on its feet,
crying out to you. It seems to offer
you its foot, saying leave now before
you drop from the heat and are left to roam
these grasslands blind. To wander with forever-ghosts
among the murmurings of crows who work the dirt
of all you were and are and promise to be.

Laramie Says

glass beret
      —Kitasono Katué

You have broken the glass beret
across scores of the unanointed

and have eaten those crusts
which, like bark, imitated skin.

The road home to Laramie
is shouted through the streets

of Laramie where your voice
resembles the terrible leaf.

Now the chiropractor drops
his skeletal dust on some ranch

near the kicking hooves,
and the Medicine Bows

extinguish their snow among pokers
stacked by the sheep sheds.

You say, *Bread is black. Wear it
like a hat.* You've been told

you're the toast of the town,
that you should certainly return,

have heard in your spleen
a braid of shiny hair

destroying the dust,
inciting the leaves.

Lambing

Time was too long each winter. Each spring,
death clung to our tongue. Just below
it milled failure and success: lambing seasons
that arrived to survive, the job
that finally paid, the art of making love
even when we felt less than whole. We kept hearing
the past, when the Bible would fly off the table
at a moment's drink. That the dog's sound
sleep meant mining activity along the Big Laramie
River had not lasted past 1882. A hundred years
of lack dread-fed the day. She said something
or other. He heard *something something something*.
We cattle-swung regret, lumbering in
from the bunchgrass, our heads jostling side to side,
mumbling as if our mouths meant medicine.
The Denver Mint, too, was south. The silver had long run
out downstream from what our grandmothers hoped
could be permanent indoor plumbing. Sure, we'd flourished
far enough to eliminate inside, but now the odor
of a hundred years of struggle lingered long minutes
in us, crawling up the wall. We tried to take
walks, even when it rained, the sound
on our roofs a rustle of restless regret
keeping us locked in homes whose walls
displayed rows of fading photos
of how we'd aged. Each smile, each head tilt
given on cue, somehow meant falling through
the boards of the barnwood floor. How we thought
the present was here to stay. How our tongues
held dread. How a spring lamb,
unsteady and weak, might bleat defeat.

Return from Durango

    Down a steep incline
                here, in Livermore,
        summer blisters everything
            but my wrist

How is it that I have protected the soft spots
    with books   mirrors   collections of dust,
        with the sleep of animal fur
            as blessèd people-light?

    I have left the gut-slinging
        and table-turning
             in Durango, along with
all the possible   pain   I have loved

        it   all
        and I have left   nearly every bit
            of it

        rotting here, at home now, in the gravel—the dead
baby rabbit that is   no more   than six
        inches of sleep, its still
            body   its slit
        eye   slit   shut

with the perfect performance of sun   permanently
    riding the cloud ponies of this place
  into perpetual burn
If I bring this stranger home   place it in my bed

        it would still
                rot
     If I leave it for the owl   whom I love
          and hope returns

          death feeds
              at least
                    a little while
            long

If I give into the profundity of its tiny rabbit grasp
                            shocked in mid-stride
              before it was hit
                   with the full force of wind
   that blew the soul clear out   of its belly

            it would
      grasp me   and does   hard
          where it hurts

It is true I have asked for   this life
        in a West   wild
    as difficult sunrise on a grave,   burning
          the cold snow   of the high country
                down into drinkable
              repair
                 I need
most what in needing me allows me to lose
                            myself
          in the larger measure
              of now

                    Please don't think me a fool, though
I likely am   Durango is no longer the Strater Hotel,
      no longer   stiff shots
of whiskey and a beer   back,
        no longer   stiff shots   of bullet holes
in the ceiling of the Diamond Belle   Saloon
                    but is a good day's   drive
        south   of every border

        it seems   The thinning between
rabbit-snatch and blur   word and

        fur   The carefully thriven, stitched
                in places I dare not

                        disturb

              I am
      with it,   that border
              south,   that space within
my internal whirl,   in elk bellies
                        of the northern Rockies
          in the healing   waters
              of Pagosa Springs
                  in the silver-heavy San Juans,
as home   now   is with me
              bitten on this gravel   road
      by six   baby inches
                        of fur
by the practical   work of ants

    that kill the killing

                              into a life less
                              meant,

    as they work and   work
                              the body
                                            clean

If We Could Ask Water
to Finally Forgive Water

A word opens
A mouth becomes itself
In the letting go
Cottonwoods conspire with cattails
Bending into them
Bending back the word
Our world in autumn mountain air
Is a world of fog
For most midnights, morning is a foreign invasion
Camped on the hillside like the Macedonian hordes
The armies of the night conflate into one long darkness
Sometimes dark / sometimes darker
Maybe there are stars in my mouth
Maybe there's an Earth opening
In the tree bark
Part of my heart
Maybe there are people finally respecting people
We know the coming of the long winter
The tents the prairie grass the sod huts
On the Colorado plains near Timnath near Severance
Where sentences stutter in whiplash wind
And commas refuse to come
You could hear our pride beginning to dissolve
Out there with the rabbitbrush and witch hazel
You could feel for the forest tribes for the stick people
The sentences without end
You could ask water to finally forgive itself for flowing
Indiscriminately

Year in / year out
Every eagle, every hawk feather arrives as a complex
Math problem, an algebra of air
A geometry of mouths
Where our breath is only a fraction of the wind
Triangulating a past
Toward which we incline
And we know the slow count of the darkening days
Marching toward winter
For most afternoons, evening is a dampening down
That alarms us
If we bled into one another we'd realize we are as similar
As a stand of trees and a river
By which we'd forever intertwine and *be* one another
We'd be root systems, say, sharing water
A word opening in ways which lend it relevance
And give moistness unto the throat
Our mornings on this autumn
Mountain are mornings mostly of fog and bits of almost-rain
Somehow the sun comes to pierce most days
And cloudburst our heart
With a scorching sound
And the tip of its flaming sword

What I Learned

This mountain allows me not to speak
for days and days, maybe longer. Sometimes
I get very quiet and think I might want to dissolve—
to dislodge those parts that hurt
and hold me back. I could slip
into the river, follow the fox, who paused
on our dirt road this evening and looked long
and lovingly into me
among torrents of touch, scraps
of could be and can't, and hard holdings
of the moon. I'd love to scratch and hollow out
the earth with her, lie with the fox
in her den—both of us digging the dirt
for warm bits of starlight—pet her gently,
whimpering back the wind, and tell her
all the things I never learned
while being human.

The Rain That Doesn't Reach the Ground

Sometimes it doesn't rain
   even when it rains. Sometimes

clouds asketh of us to allow ourselves

to pour down, pour out of ourselves the lost
   parts we have been searching for and have

      just found. Yes, I've made mistakes. Sure

as the last breath I'm certain
   to one day take. Count the headstones

we've slept on with our mounting human fears.

Find upon them the names
   we have torn apart. The names we have

      unwittingly inscribed unto ourselves:

Slow Grower. Ruminator. I Never
   Reached the Sun. Sometimes we reach

without reaching, crying out into the sycamores.

The oaks. Sometimes we don't grow
   even when we do. I have traveled

      a long way from here to there. From this woods

to that. I have held many
    hound dogs. Held my place

on Earth. Snout-driven and strong.

Kissed *this* dearth of dirt. *That*. Allowed
    the sound of my mouth banked there

        in Indiana woods. In Colorado trees at 7,600 feet.

It is time to stand. Elevate. Stand somewhere
    between yes and no. Right and wrongly

right. All the animals we've wept sleep

soundly in us as the sleeping rain hangs
    in clouds across the Laramie Plains.

        In clouds that threaten evening but never

extend. Stand on this last piece of land.
    Remind ourselves we are here. Now.

That when the rain rains it may not

always reach the ground. That the wind
    tearing us apart can only rip into us

        so far. That the sound of our mouth

is the sound of one vowel
    beckoning another, scraping up

against our breath. One vowel

across clouds that may or may not break
    open an evening sky so wet

        we remain thrilled in the precipitating

moment. Even when the rain
    raining right in front of us

never reaches the sound

of our one true mouth. Never touches
    the ground that surrounds all the lost parts

        we are sure are waiting there to be found.

The Barn at the End of the World

What we write about is what we do not understand.
—Mary Rose O'Reilley

So, this is the beginning and end of the world.
Outside Steamboat Springs, an old barn tucked
in a wide river valley. Its thin ribs allow sunlight
to pierce them. To coax the wind. And a moon-bit breeze
inhaling and exhaling our many losses
and what our losses eventually lose. Like those barns
back in Indiana. In Linton. Bedford. In Cataract Falls.
Those hovels housing multiple hound dog
births. And the births of my burgeoning years
of yeses and nos. My near misses and what-ifs.

So, this is how the heart divides. This is how
the heart learns to yearn and ache. Driving
here to there, we see our reflection mirrored
in the river. Those waterways that flow
without end. The Yampa. The Poudre.
Even back East—to the Ohio and Wabash.
Into the Hocking Hills and Opossum
Hollow. Something is scooped out
of our lives. We see it in the hollers of Indiana.
At the bottom of a buffalo jump in Fort Collins,
Colorado. In the mirror each morning
trying to tell us, *Not so, not so.*

We thought better of our lives. *I* thought better
of *my* life. But they have followed me here

to Livermore—these lives—even
from the still point of Sorrow.
I want to capitalize every word that hurts.
I want to capitalize *My Mouth*. I want to stand
straight and bold and larger than the wind
wailing my name. To let the world
know what we say is what we are. And how
our first death is a very large book we could only
make it through the first chapter of. Our knuckles
sore to the core from beating the steering wheel
for guiding us so glidingly into the dark.

So, this is all there is to it? The beginning
and beginning of how things heal? Here,
outside Steamboat Springs, a barn wedged
into a wide river valley like a wood-slatted tomb
named only *Mail Pouch* or *Copenhagen*
but crying out, *Teach Me How Not to Hurt!*
Everything in Indiana remains parched and sore.
The sheep were right. The goats were right.
The horses and llamas too, as they stomped
the hay and tried to trick the moon into repentance,
kicking themselves in the muddling
of their own deep sleep.

Once upon a time, we were alive—
here, in Colorado, back in Indiana,
in the swimming deeps of the womb
world of cornhusks in both states.
In the fields between rivers.
The fields of yes, no, and maybe. Fields
endlessly breathing, begging us

to forgive them. To forgive
ourselves. The whole of it
and more. This barn at the end
of the bend of the world.
And cornhusks calling me to sleep again
in their silk bellies.

THROWING SALT
AT MY MOTHER

Throwing Salt at My Mother

She came again last night—
two, three dreams a week since she left
the body seven years ago.
My wife and I were hauling the Indiana oak
beneath which we'd gotten married, lugging it
with us all the way to Colorado, planting it here
on our mountain. And my mother
praised us, recalling for me an old photo
of her and me beneath that tree when I was five,
maybe six, the jeans I was meant to grow into
rolled at the cuffs, knees worn
from playing marbles. The sky was piercingly blue
and tornado-green at the same time—shifting,
it seemed, whenever I glanced at the slash pile
at the edge of the woods where we were told
to avoid the snakes. The hounds were restless,
a gangly blue-speckled pup running into my arms,
whining and whimpering for me to adopt it.
Dark across my heart, I knew the world could not
keep going on. That my breath would one day
cease. I had inconceivably reached
my sixty-ninth year. And all the hours of weeping,
of feeling less than whole, stood like stone
figures at the opening of a tomb. Fog
like talus caves settling. Woodsmoke
clouding my mouth. And still, I wanted to live.
And my mother wanted me to have that tree,
leaning into me, saying, *Bring it inside near the willow,
honey, already growing in your chest*. And all I knew

was how little I *knew*. How the crowded years
of the leafy growth of my brain
had brought me only a bit of shade, a slip
of shelter from the rain. Somehow, there were piles of salt
at the base of the tree, stacked like tiny Shinto temples,
circling it. I reached for them and began
throwing handfuls at my mother, saying,
I therefore commit your body to this tree.
Leaf to leaf, branch to branch.
We come from salt, and to salt we return.
It made so little sense, but I knew she needed
to absorb the salt, absorb whatever I threw at her.
That she was my mother drawing me back in.
That I would give birth to her
always, night after night
in my sleep.

NOTES

Epigraphs

Weather Notebook (opening epigraph), from Mount Washington Observatory, https://mountwashington.org/sunrise-and-virga/.

William Stafford (opening epigraph), from "A Glass Face in the Rain," *A Glass Face in the Rain: New Poems*, Harper & Row, Publishers, 1982.

Jim Wayne Miller ("Only the Wind"), from "Winter Days," *The Mountains Have Come Closer*, Appalachian Consortium Press, 1980.

Eric Pankey, ("Prayer to the Red Fox Who Appeared Near the August Blue Moon, 2023"), from "After Li Ho," *Dismantling the Angel*, Parlor Press, 2014.

Richard Hugo ("Drinking Coffee at the Only Bar in Dixon Because Richard Hugo, James Welch, and J. D. Reed Had Whiskey There"), from "Hot Springs," *The Lady in Kicking Horse Reservoir*, W. W. Norton & Company, Inc., 1973.

Theodore Roosevelt ("Graves at Victor"), from his comments in Victor, Colorado, March 1901, quoted on the Victor Heritage Society website: https://www.victorheritagesociety.com/theodore-roosevelts-chaotic--triumphant-visits-to-victor.html, VictorHeritageSociety.com, 2024.

Richard Hugo ("When I Wept the Animal"), from "Bear Paw," *The Lady in Kicking Horse Reservoir*, W. W. Norton & Company, Inc., 1973.

Kenneth Rexroth ("Nocturne of the Western Night"), from "Andree Rexroth," *The Collected Shorter Poems*, New Directions Publishing Corporation, 1966. (The epigraph is drawn from the first of three poems with this title.)

William Stafford ("Back There in the Old Days"), from *The Way It Is: New & Selected Poems*, Graywolf Press, 1998.

Kitasono Katué ("Laramie Says"), from the book title *Glass Beret: The Selected Poems of Kitasono Katué*, translated by John Solt, Morgan Press, 1995.

Mary Rose O'Reilley ("The Barn at the End of the World"), from the book title *The Barn at the End of the World: The Apprenticeship of a Quaker, Buddhist Shepherd*, Milkweed Editions, 2000.

TEXTUAL NOTES

In "Me. Mine. Moist. Exposed in the Medicine Bows," the opening line, "Love to whatever is loved," is from Jack Spicer, "Surrealism," *My Vocabulary Did This to Me: The Collected Poetry of Jack Spicer*, edited by Peter Gizzi and Kevin Killian, Wesleyan University Press, 2008.

In "Coyote Crossing the Road," the passage, "With nineteen / recognized subspecies, the coyote / is many animals at once," is a near verbatim adaptation of a sentence from Gary Turbak (text) and Alan Carey (photographs), *Twilight Hunters: Wolves, Coyotes & Foxes*, Northland Publishing, 1987.

In "More Palomino, Please," the poem's title is drawn from Marilyn Krysl's second book of poetry, *More Palomino, Please, More Fuchsia*, Cleveland State University Poetry Center, 1980.

"The Agony of the Leaves": In this poem and in the earlier "Drinking Tea in Mountain Moonlight, Trying to Think Only of Tea," I refer to the concept of "the agony of the leaves." It comes from Helen Gustafson's book *The Agony of the Leaves: The Ecstasy of My Life with Tea*, cited in Frank Hadley Murphy's marvelous work *The Spirit of Tea*, Sherman Asher Publishing, 2008. He says, "I could never relate to the use of this phrase [with regard to the moment boiling water is poured over the leaves] . . . because I have always felt that tea rejoices in its reunion with water. If there were any pain or agony in the life of a tea leaf, it would most likely be at the point when the leaf is first separated from its mother, when it is first plucked or torn from the bush" (38).

In "The Death of Nikola Tesla," the phrase, "Vallejo said nothing, fingering, instead, the outline of his skeleton through a suit coat that had grown too large, a skeleton he had washed every day," is a reference to César Vallejo's line, "wash your skeleton every day," from the poem beginning "Let the millionaire go naked . . .," *The Complete Posthumous Poetry*, translated by Clayton Eshleman and José Rubia Barcia, University of California Press, 1978.

In "501 Words West of Wichita," the quotes on ginseng (*Moles is awful bad on 'sang* and *They'll eat the root, a mole will*) are from Wallace Moore, quoted (without the apostrophe for "sang") in "Ginseng," *Foxfire 3*, edited by Eliot Wigginton, et. al., Anchor Books (Random House), 1975.

"This Hour" includes the Kenneth Rexroth line *All this will never be again* (from "The Wheel Revolves"), as well as the lines *brain . . . worried and tired* and *Suffused with light* (from "GIC to HAR"), *The Collected Shorter Poems*, New Directions Publishing Corporation, 1966.

In "The Compassionate Darkness," the opening line, "The compassionate darkness came in," is from Rachel Peden, *Rural Free: A Farmwife's Almanac of Country Living*, Alfred A. Knopf, 1961.

"Thinking of Bai Juyi on Yet Another Day of Wind in Colorado" includes reference to Burton Watson and Arthur Waley, both of whom have translated the poems of Bai Juyi (*pinyin*) under his name previously rendered by Wade-Giles as Po Chü-I. The poem explores in part the differences between the modern *pinyin* spelling of names and the antiquated Wade-Giles spelling. Thus, I have intentionally referred to Tao Yuanming, or Tao Qian (both *pinyin*), as T'ao Ch'ien (Wade-Giles) to emphasize the previous confusion of the poem's speaker. The poem also mentions some of Bai Juyi's children, including his daughter Golden Bells (809–811 C.E.) and his first son, A-ts'ui (*circa* 830–831 C.E.). As context for his many losses, and although not mentioned in the poem, his daughter A-lo (Lo-erh), born in 816 C.E., was his only child to survive into maturity.

The "Somnambulist" sections are dedicated to my friend Eric Baus—my favorite somnambulist!

ACKNOWLEDGMENTS

I want to thank the editors of the following magazines in which some of these poems, or their previous versions, first appeared:

AGNI Online: "Throwing Salt at My Mother"

The Bitter Oleander: "Dream in Which Frank Waters Is My Mother"

Boulevard: "A Theory of Taxidermy"

Calibanonline: "Me. Mine. Moist. Exposed in the Medicine Bows"

Canyon Voices: "Brain-Tanning the Hides" and "Coyote Crossing the Road"

Clade Song: "Ghost Town Train Stop on the 'Old Prairie Dog Express' of the Burlington & Missouri River Railroad" (under the title, "The Pawnee Buttes"), "Prayer to the Red Fox Who Appeared Near the August Blue Moon, 2023," "When Lightning Bugs Become the Stars," and "When Our Breath Overlaps with Ghosts"

Columbia Poetry Review: "The Death of Nikola Tesla"

Denver Quarterly: "The Mining Camps of the Mouth"

Descant (Canada): "Big Timber, 1998" (under the title, "Big Timber")

Eunoia: "Abandoned Cabin" and "Winter Almanac"

Flying Island: "At the Pawnee National Grasslands"

Four Way Review: "Lambing"

Gargoyle: "Dream in Which Georgia O'Keeffe Is My Father" (audio recording), "Drinking Tea in Mountain Moonlight, Trying to Think Only of Tea" (audio recording), and "Laramie Says"

Hamilton Stone Review: "Dead Grouse" and "Nocturne of the Western Night"

High Plains Register: "The Long Death of Doc Holliday"

The Indianapolis Review: "Only the Wind"

Lake Effect: "Drinking Coffee at the Only Bar in Dixon Because Richard Hugo, James Welch, and J. D. Reed Had Whiskey There"

Map Points: "The Last Jump"

Midwest Quarterly: "Now That the Owls Have Gone" and "Tell Me"

North American Review: "Beneath the Medicine Moon," "Driving Across the Great Plains," and "Spoken Into"

Talisman: "501 Words West of Wichita"

Several of the poems in this book also appeared for the first time in a "bus-ticket" pamphlet, *Poems of the West*, designed and published by Bob & Susan Arnold of Longhouse Publishers: "Dream in Which John Haines and I Homestead Together in Alaska," "Driving All Night from Here to There

Is Sometimes Nowhere at All," "Early Autumn Darkness, Livermore, Colorado," "Lone Owl," "New Moon, October," "Train from Denver to Grand Junction," and "When I Wept the Animal"

I also want to thank the following venues, in which some of the preceding pieces were subsequently reprinted:

Litscapes: Collected U.S. Writings 2015: "501 Words West of Wichita"

Verse Daily: "The Mining Camps of the Mouth"

A few of these poems previously appeared in the chapbook *The Mining Camps of the Mouth*, winner of the 2012 New Michigan Press Chapbook Contest.

I also want to acknowledge the Indiana Arts Commission for an Individual Artist's Fellowship (2011) and Indiana University-Purdue University Fort Wayne for a 2011 summer faculty research grant, both of which contributed to the writing of this book.

Finally, I offer great thanks to my wife, Mary Ann Cain, for all we share in work and love. John Bradley, you are my best and most devoted reader. My poetry is continuously nourished by the care and attention of several other friends as well, especially Eric Baus, Michelle Comstock, Ray Gonzalez, Patrick Lawler, Roger Mitchell, John Olson, Paul B. Roth, Geoffrey Rubinstein, Lawrence R. Smith, Tony Trigilio, and Lisa and John Zimmerman. Who could ask for better companions on the poetic path than my wife and these generous friends? I bow to you all with deep gratitude for your love and support.

ABOUT THE AUTHOR

GEORGE KALAMARAS, former Poet Laureate of Indiana (2014–2016), is Professor Emeritus of English at Purdue University Fort Wayne, where he taught for thirty-two years. He is the author of many collections of poetry. He has also published a critical study on Western language theory and the Eastern wisdom traditions, *Reclaiming the Tacit Dimension: Symbolic Form in the Rhetoric of Silence* (State University of New York Press, 1994). He is the recipient of numerous grants and awards, the most recent of which is the 2024 Indiana Book Award for Poetry for his 2023 book from Dos Madres Press, *To Sleep in the Horse's Belly: My Greek Poets and the Aegean Inside Me*. George and his wife, writer Mary Ann Cain, have nurtured beagles in their home for thirty years, first Barney, then Bootsie, and now Blaisie. George, Mary Ann, and Blaisie divide their time between Fort Wayne, Indiana, and Livermore, Colorado, in the mountains northwest of Fort Collins. They are in the process of moving to Colorado, where they will soon be living full-time.

Other books by George Kalamaras
published by Dos Madres Press

Luminous in the Owl's Rib (2019)

We Slept the Animal:
Letters from the American West (2021)

To Sleep in the Horse's Belly:
My Greek Poets and the Aegean Inside Me (2023)

For the full Dos Madres Press catalog:
www.dosmadres.com

www.ingramcontent.com/pod-product-compliance
Lightning Source LLC
LaVergne TN
LVHW040144080526
838202LV00042B/3016